ALCOHOL

Judy Monroe

—The Drug Library—

ENSLOW PUBLISHERS, INC.

44 Fadem Road	P.O. Box 38
Box 699	Aldershot
Springfield, N.J. 07081	Hants GU12 6BP
U.S.A.	U.K.

Library of Congress Cataloging-in-Publication Data

Monroe, Judy.
    Alcohol / Judy Monroe.
        p. cm. — (The Drug Library)
    ISBN 0-89490-470-1
    1. Alcoholism—United States—Juvenile literature. 2. Alcoholism—United
States—Prevention—Juvenile literature. 3. Drinking of alcoholic beverages—United
States—Juvenile literature. 4. Teenagers—United States—Alcohol use—Juvenile
literature. [1. Alcohol. 2. Alcoholism.]
    I. Title. II. Series.
HV5066.M66 1994   93-28607
362.29'2—dc20   CIP
                                                             AC

Printed in the United States of America

10 9 8 7 6 5

Illustration Credits: Al-Anon Family Group Headquarters, Inc., 76; Alcohol,
Drug Abuse, and Mental Health Administration, U.S. Department of Health and
Human Services., 55; Illustration by Clay Bartl, 23, 57; Just Say No International,
93; Photo by Brenda Jackson, 106; Photo taken by Clay Bartl, 25, 43; Photo taken
by Judy Monroe. Photo setup by Clay Bartl, 82; Prints and Photographs Division,
Library of Congress, 12, 14, 16; Students Against Drunk Driving (SADD), 111;
The Advertising Council, 59, 85, 103.

Cover Illustration: Photo Edit, Paul Conklin.

Contents

1 Nature's Drink 5

2 Alcohol and Its Effects 19

3 The Accepted Drug 35

4 Who's an Alcoholic? 52

5 Families and Alcohol 67

6 Treatment and Prevention 79

7 Drunk Driving, Pregnancy,
and Alcohol 96

Alateen: Is It for You? 112

Glossary 115

Chapter Notes 118

Further Reading 123

Titles For Teens 124

Where to Go for Help 125

Index 127

1

Nature's Drink

The Discovery of Alcohol

Because the earliest people did not keep written records, no one knows exactly when alcoholic beverages were first discovered. But researchers believe that alcohol was man's first drug. Perhaps people living in a hot climate ate some stored dates, grapes, berries, or honey that had begun to rot. Since they were hungry, they ate the food and liked the taste. Maybe they got intoxicated or drunk from the crude alcohol that had formed.

The ancient people could not see the tiny yeast spores, cells that make alcohol. Yeasts are one-celled microorganisms. They change sugars in fruits, berries, or honey into alcohol and carbon dioxide. This process is called fermentation. Wild yeast spores are all around us in the air. Most yeasts that make alcohol and bread are called "sugar fungi" because they break down sugar into carbon dioxide and alcohol.

The word *alcohol* comes from the Arabic word "al-kohl." At

5

first, the word was used to describe a type of eyeliner that women in the Middle East wore. Later, it came to mean any exotic substance.

Over 5,000 years ago, people all over the world began making alcoholic beverages. The first beverages were beer and wine. People discovered that making simple beers and wines was rather easy and that the ingredients were easy to gather and use.

Beer and Wine

Before people used grapes to make wine, they discovered that starchy grains, such as barley, wheat, millet, and corn, could produce alcohol. Beer became the drink of common people in many parts of the world. This was because beer was easier to make than wine, and grains were less costly to grow or buy than special types of wine grapes. Also, in early times, water was often foul-tasting and unclean. Clear, unspoiled drinking water was hard to find and was considered precious. So, people often drank beer instead.

Beer actually was a food for early people. "Most modern beers are very thin, but ancient beer was a food. Fermentation added needed B vitamins and essential amino acids converted by the yeast. And yeast also deactivated several toxic compounds in the barley, making it taste better. Beer was better than bread in the sense that it also had alcohol in it," said Solomon Katz, an anthropologist at the University of Pennsylvania.[1]

The first beer was made in the Middle East. Sealed clay jars in Mesopotamia and hieroglyphics—writing in the form of pictures—in Egypt show people making beer. The process then moved to northern Europe. Here, the climate was too cold to grow grapes, and beer quickly became an important drink. Only wealthy people could afford to import wines from the warmer, southern countries of Europe and the Middle East.

Today, beer remains the national beverage of Germany, Belgium, and the Netherlands. Ale is the same as beer, except that it is made from different strains of yeast. But in Italy and France, southern European countries, wines are the national alcoholic beverages.

People in Mesopotamia and ancient Egypt were also the first to make grape wines. By about 700 B.C., wine had become the basic beverage of the Greeks. The Greek word for "to breakfast" was *akratidzomai*, meaning "to drink undiluted wine." People dipped pieces of hard bread in wine to soften it and to make it tastier. Later, people in Italy, Egypt, Greece, and Gaul (later called France) became known for their fine wines.

Other early people discovered how to make beer and wine, too. In the Far East, barley and rice were made into alcoholic beverages. These same drinks are still popular in India, Sri Lanka, the Philippines, China, and Japan. African people used corn, millet, bananas, honey, palm or bamboo sap, and many kinds of fruits to make wines and beers. Nomadic people in northern Europe and central Asia did not grow grains to use for alcoholic beverages. Instead, they fermented milk into wines.

Some early people were not exposed to and did not drink alcoholic beverages. The people of the Pacific Islands and many Native Americans in North America did not make alcoholic beverages. However, Native Americans in the southwest United States made a cactus wine.

Distilled Alcohols or Liquors

Early peoples did not leave written records of when and how

they learned to make distilled alcohols. However, the distilling process required great skill. First, a liquid such as beer or wine is boiled. The cooled vapors are condensed and concentrated. Impurities must be removed. The result: a liquid with a high alcohol content and strong taste.

In 1100 A.D. the first written account of alcohol distillation was recorded at a medical school in Salerno, Italy. Here, wine was boiled and distilled into a type of brandy. Scholars and doctors thought this new drink was really a strong medicine. A Spanish scholar called it *aqua vitae* (water of life).

For hundreds of years, only pharmacies and monasteries made these liquids, and their use was limited to treating illnesses. For example, cordials were thought to be a medicine that stimulated the heart and blood system. Today, cordials are a type of after-dinner drink.

By the 1400s, distilled alcohols or spirits were also enjoyed as a beverage by other people. The knowledge of distillation spread all over Europe. Some countries became known for their unique distilled alcohols:

- Russia—vodka, from fermented barley or potatoes
- Holland—*jenever*, or gin, from barley
- Scandinavia—*akvavit*, from fermented potatoes
- Ireland—whiskey, from barley
- Mexico—tequila, from the agave cactus

Disapproval of Drunkenness

Ancient people often drank alcoholic beverages for special events. It was part of many worship ceremonies and was used in the practice of magic and medicine. By about 1500 B.C., Egyptian doctors included beer or wine in about 15 percent of their medicines.[2]

Some religions made wine an important part of holidays or events. The Jewish people still drink wine during Passover, an important holiday that celebrates the Jews leaving slavery in Egypt. Also, adults in the family may drink wine during Friday night meals, to start the Jewish Sabbath, or day of rest. Many Christians also drink a sip of wine during their church services as a symbol of Jesus Christ's blood. Throughout history, people have lifted glasses of alcohol during births, marriages, weddings, funerals, and festivals. Friends sometimes shared drinks at home or in public places such as inns or taverns.

Along with the pleasures of alcohol came excessive drinking. Sometimes people drank too much because of contests or because they liked the effects. Some people drank to escape the unhappiness of a hard life. But the problems related to too much drinking were also recognized. The Old Testament contains warnings against too much drinking. Greek and Roman classic writings give many examples of drunkenness and the need for moderation, drinking without becoming drunk.

Various attempts to stop people from drinking to excess have been made in Greece, Italy, Egypt, Japan, China, Russia, and the United States. Throughout recorded history, people have frowned on and have tried to stop drunkenness.

Alcohol in Early America

The colonists brought alcoholic beverages to their new land and also the skills to make these beverages. The Puritans made their alcoholic beverages from apples, grapes, berries, carrots, celery, or spinach and also used various grains. They set up many public drinking places called tippling houses, for those who did not make their own alcoholic beverages. Inns and taverns also served drinks to guests and travelers.

Just as in early times, alcohol was the drink for celebrating. People served it on special occasions such as weddings, funerals, or births. Early dentists and surgeons had no drugs to put their patients to sleep before an operation. Instead, they had their patients drink to ease some of the pain or even to lose consciousness. In many highly religious homes, no alcohol was served "except for cold remedies. Hot toddy, made with liquor (usually whiskey), sugar, water, and a little lemon juice, was a common remedy. Even children might be given a small toddy when afflicted with a winter cold."[3]

By the 1700s, settlers in the northern colonies had learned to distill their local crops of rye and barley into whiskey. By 1780, people in Kentucky began making whiskey from corn. Early settlers also invented bourbon, a new distilled alcohol made from corn. Early Americans liked to drink. Nancy Nielsen writes that "in the late 1700s, President Thomas Jefferson claimed that, 'one-third of the people in the United States are killing themselves with whiskey.'[4] By 1830, Americans drank nearly three times as much alcohol per person as today.[5]

Many early Americans were drinking a lot of alcohol but did not realize it. The alcohol was in their patent medicines. These fake drugs or remedies were taken without prescriptions and often contained large amounts of alcohol. "Anyone could sell patent medicines, and Americans bought thousands of them. They wanted cures for coughs, upset stomachs, and sore backs . . . Patent medicines often claimed to cure almost everything."[6] For example, Hostetter's Bitters, a popular patent medicine during the mid-1800s, was 32 percent alcohol. The manufacturer claimed that Hostetter's Bitters was "as harmless as water from the mountain spring." Yet this liquid had been sold in Alaskan saloons and in bars and stores in the continental United States.[7]

Later immigrants also made their own alcoholic beverages. During the early 1900s, for example, people from Yugoslavia, Southern Slavs, often made their own wines. They used dandelions in the spring, and grapes, cherries, and blackberries during the summer. The Greeks, too, made homemade wines from various grapes.

American wines gained in popularity during the 1800s. In 1840, fifteen states were producing a lot of it, and the main producers were New York, Ohio, and Missouri. California wines won thirty-six medals at the 1900 Paris Exposition. However, most of its grape vines were killed by a plant disease and had to be replanted after 1933. Today, California wines are once again becoming popular.

Temperance in America

During the 1800s, the temperance movement, calling for moderation, not drinking to drunkenness, began growing. Most states had at least one temperance organization by 1832, and in 1833 the American Temperance Union formed. Early temperance supporters did not oppose drinking in moderation. They fought against drunkenness and paying workers in liquor instead of money. They also wanted alcoholic beverages to be taxed and taverns to be regulated by requiring liquor licenses.

Lyman Beecher was an early leader who wanted to temper, reduce America's drinking, by making liquor illegal. However,

Carrie A. Nation reads her Bible in a Wichita, Kansas jail. She violently opposed all alcoholic drinking. Her destructive anti-drinking methods sometimes landed her in jail.

he thought the selling and drinking of wine and beer was all right. Other people, such as Frances Willard, disagreed. She wanted to prohibit or stop the drinking of all alcohol, including wine and beer. She formed a new temperance group in 1874, the Women's Christian Temperance Union, to teach about the dangers of drinking.

Another woman named Carrie A. Nation went even further than Willard in her strong opposition to drinking. She gained a national reputation for her fearless wielding of an axe, chopping open barrels of beer and breaking whiskey bottles in taverns and saloons throughout America. She was arrested over thirty times. She died in 1911, only eight years before the start of Prohibition, which made drinking illegal.

Prohibition and Its Repeal

For years, the Anti-Saloon League and other temperance groups had encouraged the U.S. government to prohibit the sale of alcohol. In 1919, both the House of Representatives and the Senate passed the Eighteenth Amendment to the U.S. Constitution. This said that no alcohol could be manufactured, imported, exported, transported, or sold in the United States. However, the law did **not** prohibit the purchase or use of alcohol. Thirty-six states immediately approved it.

At first, the law hurt the alcohol business. Nearly 200,000 saloons went out of business during Prohibition. Liver diseases fell in the first years. Public drunkenness also declined. However, paralysis, blindness, and death became more common as people drank homemade alcohols containing poisons. Prohibition caused a large drop in the production and sale of beer, but sales of distilled spirits or hard liquor increased.

13

This woman shows her ankle flask which she used to hide illegal alcohol. Some people broke Prohibition, the U.S. law which made alcohol drinking illegal from 1919 to 1933.

Moonshining — the making of homemade whiskey — and smuggling greatly increased during Prohibition. Al Capone (1899–1947) was known as the King of Bootleg Liquor, that is, illegally manufactured alcohol. During the 1920s, he ruled all of Chicago's crime world and made huge sums of money from his illegal liquor sales. Finally, he was imprisoned in 1931.

Although many people supported the law, some broke the law by making alcohol at home or going to speakeasies to drink. Speakeasies were places where alcoholic beverages were illegally sold. Parties by middle- and upper-class people were a big hit when they would fill their bathtub with gin. Violent crimes increased due to illegal alcohol making, transport, and sales. The government could not handle all the lawbreakers, and in just three years, the prison populations had nearly doubled. People became increasingly afraid of all of the crime and violence, and began to ask that the law be repealed, or reversed.

In 1933, some fourteen years after it began, America's experiment with prohibition, which had made alcohol illegal, ended. The Twenty-first Amendment, which made alcohol sales and use legal for adults, was passed. Amendment 18, the Prohibition Amendment, has been the only amendment to the constitution ever repealed in American history.

Today's Alcohol Trends

Americans drink more today than they did before Prohibition. Beer consumption has gone from sixteen gallons to twenty-four gallons per person. Distilled spirits consumption is now at 1.5 gallons per person, compared to just over one gallon before Prohibition.[8]

15

Federal government officials destroy 749 cases of beer from
Philadelphia. Government workers could not keep up with all the
illegal alcohol made and sold during Prohibition.

One trend has changed. Before Prohibition, most alcohol in the United States was sold and drunk in public places, such as saloons. Now, almost 75 percent of all beer, wine, and distilled alcohol is sold in stores and supermarkets and drank at home or at parties.[9]

Today, more than 60 percent of all Americans drink alcoholic beverages. Most of these people drink light or moderate amounts of alcohol. Moderate drinking, as defined by the U.S. government, is no more than two average drinks per day for men and one average drink per day for women. However, moderate drinking is difficult to define because it can mean different things to different people. Also, research shows that people who drink lightly or moderately can experience alcohol-related problems, such as side effects of the interaction of alcohol with medicines, and impaired driving skills.

Currently, there are 10.5 million alcoholics in the United States. Another 8 million people are heavy drinkers.[10] Alcoholism is the number one drug problem in America today, although many people think that crack, cocaine, or other illegal drugs are the number one drug problem.[11]

Prevention through education, and treatment programs help deal with alcoholism and the possible abuse of alcohol. Most schools now offer drug and alcohol education. Public awareness has increased about the effects of drinking too much. Teens and adults are better informed, so they can choose if and when to use alcohol.

Questions For Discussion

1. People began making alcoholic beverages over 5,000 years ago. Can you think of any other foods or drinks that we still have today that were discovered long ago?

2. The word for alcohol comes from Arabic. Can you think of any other words for different foods that come from other languages?

3. Why do you think the Eighteenth Amendment, which made alcohol illegal, was a failure?

2

Alcohol and Its Effects

What Is Alcohol?

Ethyl alcohol, or ethanol, is a thin, colorless liquid with little or no odor. Alcohol has no vitamins, minerals, or nutrients. Most nutrients are lost during alcohol processing.

Most people do not drink pure alcohol. Instead, they drink beverages containing ethanol. Alcoholic beverages fall into three groups: beer, wine, and distilled spirits, such as whiskey, gin, vodka, rum, and brandy.

Manufacturers make wines from fruits, berries, honey, some vegetables, and even milk. They ferment beers from grains, including barley, wheat, corn, and rice. Distilled spirits, also known as hard liquor or spirits, are distilled from wines or beers. Distillation, a complex process, produces beverages with a higher alcohol content.

The amount of ethanol in alcoholic beverages varies:

- 2 to 8 percent in beers; most U.S. beers contain 5 to 6 percent

- 4 to 7 percent in wine coolers

- 8 to 20 percent in wines

- 40 to 50 percent in distilled spirits.

The alcoholic content of distilled spirits is also measured as "proof". One degree of proof means 0.5 percent alcohol. An 80 proof alcoholic beverage, such as vodka, is actually 40 percent alcohol.

Manufacturers sometimes add ingredients to alcoholic beverages to make various drinks. Distilled spirits, because of their high alcohol content, are often mixed with water, soda, or fruit juices. The color and taste of alcoholic beverages vary a lot, from clear, tasteless vodka to tart cranberry cordials, to golden beers.

Alcohol is high in sugar and calories. There are about 170 calories in 12 ounces of beer and 150 calories in 5 ounces of wine. Light beers contain about 112 to 140 calories. A mixed drink of alcohol, fruit juice, and soda adds up to about 300 calories.

One of the more recent drinks is the wine cooler, which tastes sweet and syrupy because of its fruit juices and sugar. Wine coolers also contain red or white wine. Their alcohol content is the same as a can of beer. Thinking that people would like a soft drink mixed with alcohol, two California businessmen invented wine coolers in 1980. In 1985 they sold their growing company to a large liquor manufacturer. Today, wine coolers are big business, with sales of over $1 billion each year.[1]

Other forms of alcohol exist but are not meant for people to drink. Gasoline mixed with alcohol (gasohol) fuels automobiles and buses. Isopropyl alcohol, or rubbing alcohol, helps soothe tired muscles. Doctors and nurses clean patients' skin with rubbing alcohol before giving shots. Many household products contain alcohol—cosmetics, paints, varnishes, and inks. Alcohol is also in antifreeze and dry-cleaning fluids.

How Alcohol Is Made

All alcohol is made the same way—from fermentation or the process of yeast changing sugars into ethyl alcohol. Different yeasts produce different alcohols. The yeasts used to make alcoholic beverages are also known as sugar fungi.

Yeast fungi are microscopic, living, one-celled plants. They do not need much oxygen and like warm temperatures and moist places to grow. Yeasts are so small that one pound of yeast contains over 3 trillion yeast cells. Bakers use one type of yeast to make breads. Other types of yeast are used to produce alcoholic beverages.

Making alcoholic beverages is a big business. In 1990, the United States produced 8 billion gallons of these beverages. Seventy-five percent of that was beer.[2]

Alcohol Metabolism

The body metabolizes, or breaks down, alcohol differently from the way it breaks down solid food. Typical alcohol metabolism occurs like this: With the first sip, alcohol briefly irritates the mouth and esophagus linings. It then flows into the stomach.

The stomach, although irritated by the alcohol, absorbs about 20 percent of it. Food in the stomach slows its absorption somewhat.

The remaining alcohol quickly moves into the small intestine, bloodstream, and heart. The heart pumps the alcohol through blood vessels to the rest of the body, including the brain. Once alcohol reaches the brain, drinkers begin to feel its effects.

It takes only a few minutes from the first sip to the moment alcohol moves into the brain. Alcohol slows down brain cells but increases the heartbeat. Alcohol is a toxin, or poison, to the body. The body tries to remove it quickly by increasing blood flow and blood pressure.

The body removes alcohol in two ways: excretion and metabolism. Only 10 percent of alcohol is excreted through urine, breath, saliva, or sweat. The other 90 percent remains in the body until enzymes, or complex proteins, in the liver break down the alcohol into water and carbon dioxide. The liver is the only organ that breaks down alcohol.

The liver can break down about one-third ounce of pure alcohol every hour. A typical liver can handle about one-half ounce of pure alcohol in about one and a half hours. The following beverages each contain about half an ounce of alcohol:

- one 12-ounce can of beer

- one 12-ounce wine cooler

- one 5-ounce glass of wine

- a drink containing 1.25 ounces of liquor, such as rum, whiskey, gin, vodka, and so on.

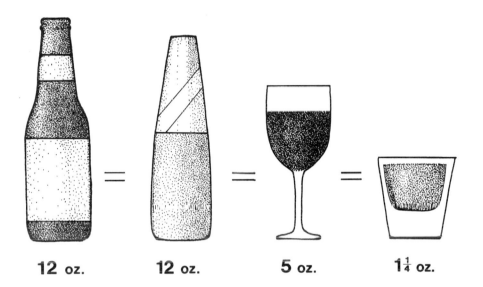

12 oz.   **12** oz.   **5** oz. $1\frac{1}{4}$ oz.

The alcohol content of all four beverages is the same.

Effects and Hazards

Alcohol affects everyone, from the first-time drinker to alcohol abusers. However, alcohol's effects are different for each person. Effects depend on a person's weight, age, sex, the type of alcohol, drinking history, and mood and expectations.

Weight. Alcohol generally affects women and teens faster than it does men because women and teenagers have smaller bodies.

Age. Alcohol affects teens and children faster than adults. This is because underage drinkers are usually smaller. Also, teens and children are still developing physically, mentally, and emotionally and so are more easily affected.

Gender. Women are affected faster than men because they have more body fat. Fat absorbs alcohol poorly, so alcohol tends to concentrate more in a woman's bloodstream.

Type of Alcohol. Carbonated alcohols such as sparkling wines, wine coolers, or champagne mixed with carbonated drinks like ginger ale, are absorbed more rapidly. Switching drinks does not affect how fast the body absorbs carbonated alcohol. The body treats all alcohol the same.

History of Alcohol Use. Tolerance is a diminished effect of the same amount of alcohol; it is developed with regular use. Tolerance builds up in chronic heavy drinkers.

Mood and Expectations. Alcohol's effects can vary, depending on the drinker's mood and expectations. Stress can cause alcohol to affect a drinker more. Because alcohol alters brain functions, drinkers may do things they might not do when sober, such as commit crimes, become suicidal, or abuse others.

Alcohol and many different drugs interact, often causing very serious reactions.

Alcohol affects more than mood and emotions. Even in low to moderate amounts, it can:

- Cause drowsiness and affect sleep. Just one drink can make for a fitful night of sleep. Alcohol affects deep sleep, which is the dream phase of sleep.

- Affect vision by relaxing the eye muscles that open and close the pupil. Drinkers thus are less able to deal with bright lights, see from the side, see some colors such as red, and track moving objects. This means drivers have problems following a moving car, person, and so on.

- Interfere with attention and memory.

- Affect sexual ability. A few drinks may lower a drinker's inhibitions about having sex. More drinks can lead to loss of feeling and an inability to have sex.

- Reduce sensitivity to pain, taste, and odor.

- Trigger allergies. Between 0.5 and 1.7 million Americans are allergic to ingredients in beer, wine, or distilled spirits. Alcohol is only one ingredient in alcoholic beverages. Others include grains, yeast, malt, fruit, molasses, saccharin, coloring agents such as Yellow Dye #5, and preservatives such as sulfites. Allergic reactions are often swift: wheezing, itching, hives, headaches, stomach pains, shock, and even death can occur.

- Interact with other drugs. Even one drink,

combined with other drugs, often multiplies or exaggerates the effects of both drugs. Doctors and pharmacists warn not to mix alcohol with over one hundred other drugs, including some sold without a prescription. The following are examples of drugs that do not mix with alcohol: aspirin or other drugs for headaches and arthritis, barbiturates or sedatives, antihistamines or other allergy medicines, tranquilizers, some antibiotics, and diabetic drugs.

Getting Drunk

Alcohol is a powerful depressant drug. It slows down and can even block nerve cells. In small amounts, such as one or two drinks slowly sipped, a person may feel pleasant and relaxed, or drowsy. This is because alcohol causes nerve cells to slow down messages to the brain. Alcohol depresses almost every brain function, from balance to breathing; it also lowers body temperature.

For some people, even a small amount of alcohol, such as one beer or glass of wine, causes intoxication or drunkenness. Young people or those over age fifty cannot tolerate as much alcohol as other age groups. Their livers are less efficient at breaking down alcohol. Drunk people usually undergo behavior changes. Some become depressed. Others get reckless, rude, loud, tell lots of jokes, or cry or giggle constantly.

If drinking continues, speech, vision, balance, and judgment are affected. If a lot of alcohol is consumed, the drinker could become drunk, nauseated, sleepy, or lose consciousness. He or she could also vomit because of powerful contractions of the stomach valve. This is the stomach's way of keeping poisonous amounts of alcohol from moving to other body parts.

A drinker can die from drinking too much alcohol too fast. This is called binge drinking, which means drinking five or more drinks in less than an hour. About two hundred deaths result each year from binge drinking or alcohol poisoning. Many of these deaths are of teens.

Sobering Up and Hangovers

What will sober up someone who is drunk? There are many myths, but **none** of these will help:

- drinking coffee or tea. One study found that drinking coffee after having one or two drinks slowed down driving responses more than drinking alcohol alone.

- taking amphetamines or other stimulants.

- cold showers.

- eating sugar.

- big gulps of fresh, cold air or oxygen.

- exercising.

No one has found a quick way to get sober. Time is the only cure. The body takes about three hours to break down one ounce of alcohol. Sobering-up rates vary with a person's body weight, health, and drinking experience.

After drinking, some people wake up with a hangover. A hangover is actually a mild withdrawal from alcohol. When a person drinks, the body adjusts to having alcohol in its tissues, but by morning the alcohol is going or is gone, and the body reacts.

Hangover symptoms can last from several hours to several days. Typical hangover symptoms include light and sound sensitivity, fatigue, upset stomach, shakiness or muscle weakness, and a headache. Headaches occur because alcohol enlarges the blood vessels in the head. The mirror may reflect a puffy face and blurry, puffy eyes. A dry mouth and thirst are also common because alcohol causes the body to lose water.

Folk remedies for hangovers are many and ancient. In medieval times, the School of Salerno in Italy recommended:

> If an evening of wine does you in,
>
> More the next morning will be medicine.[3]

However, we know now that more drinking will not cure hangovers. The only cure is time to bring the body back to a drug-free state. To ease hangover pain, doctors recommend aspirin, rest, solid food, and fruit juices or water.

Chronic Heavy Drinking

Over time, heavy drinking can lead to severe health problems. Alcohol can affect every organ system in the body.

Brain Damage. Heavy alcohol consumption is a well-documented cause of brain damage, according to a 1990 report by the National Institute of Alcohol Abuse and Alcoholism.[4] Alcohol abuse is linked to memory loss, depression, anxiety, seizures, blackouts, and hallucinations. During blackouts, drinkers do not actually lose consciousness but cannot remember what happened during a drinking episode. Chronic alcohol abuse damages brain and nervous system cells, perhaps permanently.

Heart Damage. Alcohol can affect the heart muscle so that the heart may degenerate, scar and enlarge, or beat irregularly. It can also raise blood pressure and heart rate. This places a great demand on the heart and increases the risk of stroke or heart attack.

Liver Damage. Heavy drinking can severely damage the liver, causing fatty liver, alcoholic hepatitis, and cirrhosis. All three diseases can occur at the same time in one person. About 15 to 35 percent of moderate to heavy drinkers develop extra fat in their livers. Then their livers cannot process alcohol or other foods as fast. Fatty liver disease kills over 1,000 people each year. However, if people stop drinking, their fatty livers will heal over time.

Even occasional drinkers can get alcoholic hepatitis, a painful liver inflammation. It usually lasts one to three weeks, with nausea, vomiting, stomach pain, swollen stomach, and fever. It can even cause death. But it is reversible if people stop drinking.

Cirrhosis, a permanent, dangerous disease, kills liver cells. This disease slows the blood flow through the liver. Eventually, the liver could fail. Over 14,000 people die each year from cirrhosis. It is the ninth leading cause of death in the United States.[5]

Pancreatitis. The pancreas is a small organ in the upper stomach. Pancreatitis, inflammation of the pancreas, is a serious illness. It causes vomiting, stomach pain, and nausea. About 40 percent of people with pancreatitis are alcoholics.

Cancer. Because alcohol affects the immune system, it increases the risk of cancers, especially of the mouth, throat, liver, or bladder. Studies show an increased risk for breast cancer in women alcoholics. Alcohol is a factor in over 7,000 cases of cancer each year.

AIDS. In 1992, the U.S. Centers for Disease Control estimated:

- one million Americans have the human immunodeficiency virus (HIV)

- at least 40,000 new HIV infections occur among adults and teens each year

- 20 percent of all people with acquired immunodeficiency syndrome (AIDS) are between the ages of 20 and 29. Many were infected with HIV (which usually becomes AIDS) when they were teens. HIV infection and AIDS is the sixth leading cause of death among 15- to 24-year olds in the United States.

Research shows that alcohol injures the immune system, the system that protects the body from disease. Heavy drinkers suffer more infections and cancers than nonalcoholics. This may mean that heavy drinkers could increase their chances of getting HIV if exposed to it; and, if a drinker already has HIV, alcohol could increase the risk of his or her developing AIDS.

The U.S. Office for Substance Abuse finds that drinking can lower inhibitions about having sex or practicing safe sex, which puts drinkers at greater risk of getting HIV. Among all teens who drink, 16 percent use condoms less often after drinking. Among sexually active teens, those who drink five or more drinks each day are nearly three times less likely to use condoms. This increases their risk of getting HIV.

Malnutrition. Alcoholics or chronic heavy drinkers may starve because they often prefer drinking to eating. Alcohol interferes with the body's use of vitamins and minerals. It blocks

31

the body's ability to absorb vitamins C and A, resulting in anemia and reduced resistance to disease. Doctors often find chronic alcohol abusers low in potassium, magnesium, calcium, folic acid, and thiamine. The following table lists the results of these deficiencies.

LOSS OF...	CAN CAUSE...
Potassium	Muscle weakness and irregular heartbeats.
Magnesium	Weakened bones, poor muscle contraction, poor use of food by the body.
Calcium	Double the loss of normal calcium excretion, which could lead to weakened bones.
Folic acid	Anemia, hair loss, skin changes, decreased healing of the skin, decreased sense of taste.
Thiamine	Muscle degeneration, heart irregularities, weight loss, and fatigue.

Stomach and ulcer problems. Because alcohol irritates the stomach lining, heavy alcohol use can cause heartburn, upset stomach, and stomach inflammation. It increases the risk of ulcers and makes existing ulcers worse.

Osteoporosis. Heavy drinking impairs calcium absorption. This increases the risk of osteoporosis, also known as brittle bone disease. Osteoporosis causes bone to soften and break easily. The body needs calcium to build and repair bone. Osteoporosis affects 25 million Americans, usually those over 50 years old.

32

Alcoholism

The National Council on Alcoholism defines alcoholism as:

> A chronic, progressive, and potentially fatal disease characterized by tolerance and physical dependency or organ changes, or both. Generally, alcoholism is repeated drinking that causes trouble in the drinker's personal, professional, or family life. When they drink, alcoholics can't always predict when they'll stop, how much they'll drink, or what the consequences of their drinking will be. Denial of the negative effects alcohol has in their lives is common in alcoholics and those close to them.[6]

Alcohol is the most widely used and destructive drug in America today. About 8 million Americans are problem drinkers.[7] Another 10.5 million are alcoholics or chronic heavy drinkers.[8] No cure exists for alcoholism.

If untreated, alcoholism can kill an alcoholic. The disease can be stopped by never again drinking alcohol. Alcoholics who stop drinking are called recovering alcoholics. Many will eventually heal from the physical damage caused by their drinking.

Alcoholism is the third leading cause of early death, behind cancer and heart disease. At least three out of every one hundred deaths in the United States are alcohol-related. This adds up to 110,000 alcohol-related deaths each year.[9]

Questions For Discussion

1. Many heavy drinkers and alcoholics also smoke, and this increases their chances of developing some types of cancer. Can you think of some of these cancer types?

2. Why do you think food in the stomach slows down alcohol absorption?

3. Many people think that distilled spirits are more dangerous than beer or wine. Why do you think people believe this?

3
The Accepted Drug

Early American Attitudes

Americans have long celebrated special events with alcohol. Explorers, colonists, and the Puritans brought alcohol to the new nation. The colonists drank at home or with friends for special occasions, such as births and marriages. Men, women, and children drank. However, drunkenness soon became a problem in the young colonies.

The colonists viewed drunkenness as the sinful, immoral behavior of the weak-willed. Many people believed that alcoholics chose to be drunk.[1] Laws were passed from the 1600s to the 1800s to deal with drunkenness. For example, Virginia colonists tried to outlaw drunkenness in 1632. Their attempt soon failed. Instead, more drinking places sprang up.

After the American Revolution, drinking continued to move from the home to taverns and saloons. Men drank and socialized there. Beer and whiskey cost less after the Revolution because England no longer collected alcohol taxes. Since alcohol was cheaper and more available, more people drank. The number of alcoholics grew. In 1851, the average American drank seven gallons of pure alcohol a year.

In a later attempt to stop alcohol abuse, Prohibition became American law in 1920. At first, the law appeared to work. The number of alcoholics decreased in the early years. However, by the time the law was reversed in 1933, some Americans had openly disobeyed it. The day Prohibition ended, an excited crowd broke down the front door of the Boston Licensing Board so they could get beer licenses.

During the 1930s, alcohol use became glamorized in the movies. Famous male movie stars, such as Humphrey Bogart and Gary Cooper, drank in their films. Living room scenes displayed costly crystal decanters filled with liquors and the host mixing drinks for guests. Businessmen drank during lunches out, and in their offices, they pulled whiskey bottles from their desk drawers.

Some authors had their characters drink during business lunches and also get drunk during parties. Of the first six Americans to win the Nobel Prize for literature, five—Sinclair Lewis, Eugene O'Neill, William Faulkner, Ernest Hemingway, and John Steinbeck—were alcoholics.

Due to alcohol's glamor, availability, and low cost, alcoholism and drunk driving increased after Prohibition. Alcoholism was not yet defined as a disease or medical problem. Doctors offered little help to those trying to stop drinking. Few alcohol treatment programs existed.

Back in 1892, Dr. Franklin Clum, a New York doctor, wrote, "The time has come for a study of inebriety [drunkenness] from a medical standpoint, and when it is treated as a special disease, its curability will be found equal to any other disease."[2] Before Dr. Clum's prediction could come true, American attitudes toward alcoholism had to change a lot.

Changing Attitudes

The first major attitude change toward alcoholism came in 1935. Bill Wilson, an often-unemployed alcoholic, was finally able to stop drinking. He wanted to help other alcoholics stop drinking by using his methods and to "make them see alcoholism as a progressive disease of the mind, body and soul, a disease for which there was no physical 'cure,' but death or insanity."[3]

Together with Dr. Robert Smith, a doctor and recovering alcoholic, Bill Wilson founded Alcoholics Anonymous (AA). Today, AA is a worldwide group that offers mutual support and a twelve-step recovery program from alcohol. Its members stay away from drinking, one day at a time.

During the 1930s, Yale University began publishing a scientific magazine on alcohol research. The Yale Plan Clinic was started to diagnose and treat alcoholics. Also coming out of Yale was the National Council on Alcoholism. Founded in 1944, the council still provides information and education to people about alcohol and alcoholism.

Another major step occurred in 1956 when the American Medical Association (AMA) recognized alcoholism as a disease. The AMA has since revised its definition twice, in 1966 and 1990.

During the 1960s and 1970s, many Americans focused on abuses of other drugs, such as cocaine, marijuana, and heroin. The federal government spent millions of dollars to stop these drugs from spreading across America. Yet alcoholism became a growing problem for many more people. Researchers in the 1960s estimated that 5 million Americans were alcoholics.

The federal government finally acknowledged alcoholism as "a major public health problem" and in 1971 created the National Institute on Alcohol Abuse and Alcoholism (NIAAA).[4] The institute sponsors alcohol research, training, education, and treatment programs.

Money to start the NIAAA came from the Comprehensive Alcohol Abuse and Alcoholism Prevention, Treatment, and Rehabilitation Act of 1970. With this new law, the United States government now recognized alcoholism as a disease that required treatment. The law also protected alcoholics from discrimination when applying for jobs. In 1973, the United States passed the Federal Rehabilitation Act. This law defined alcoholism as a handicap and prohibited discrimination against anyone with a handicap. For example, alcoholics have equal rights to public housing.

In the early 1970s, the NIAAA completed a study to determine the number of alcoholics in the United States. According to its study, the number now was at 9 million.

During the 1970s, many new public and private alcoholism treatment services opened. Each state started alcohol and drug abuse services, including alcohol information, education, and treatment. Community mental health centers that received federal government money also began alcohol services. One of the biggest changes occurred when health insurance companies began paying for some alcohol treatment.

Along with a team of doctors and nurses, a new counselor appeared: the alcohol counselor or therapist. These essential people help alcoholics through treatment. Today, education and training on alcoholism and treatment is widely available for the many kinds of professionals who treat and help alcoholics.

Problems Caused by Alcohol

Alcoholism is the number one drug abuse problem among American youth. "Of all the substances Americans are likely to abuse or become addicted to, alcohol is far and away the leader—particularly among teenagers."[5]

Alcohol is the most widely used and destructive drug in America today. In the United States, alcohol accounts for about 975,000 deaths each year from alcohol-related traffic accidents, alcohol-related murders, suicides, and non-motor-vehicle accidents. This is 50 percent of all auto deaths, 60 percent of all drownings, 70 to 80 percent of all deaths in fires, and 85 percent of liver deaths. The financial cost of alcohol abuse is also high—$136 billion is spent dealing with the effects of alcoholism and related problems. And there are 76 million Americans who are or have been affected by alcohol abuse.

Suicide and alcohol are linked. From 7 to 21 percent of all alcoholics commit suicide. Just over two-thirds of all suicide attempts are alcohol-related. Suicide is the second-leading cause of death in teens under eighteen and people over sixty-five. No one knows how many of the teen suicides are alcohol-related.

Current Alcohol Use in America

Each year, the average American adult drinks 2.75 gallons of distilled spirits, 2.77 gallons of wine, and 30.4 gallons of beer. More than ten million Americans are alcoholics. Over eight million more are heavy drinkers. About 60 percent of Americans who drink are light to moderate drinkers. Moderate drinkers, according to the U.S. government, are defined as men who drink no more than two average drinks per day and women who drink no more than one average drink per day. These guidelines exclude people under the age of twenty-one, women who are pregnant or are trying to have children, people who plan to drive or operate machines, people taking medication, and recovering alcoholics

Alcohol is an accepted part of everyday life for some people. It is easy to find. In some parts of the United States, grocery stores and liquor stores are found next to each other or are combined into one store. Many grocery stores sell beer. Alcohol is served at ballparks, concerts, and many restaurants. People drink alcohol after work, during a meal, and at parties.

Americans continue to give alcohol a good image. Television programs and movies show stars drinking, having a good time, and being successful and popular. However, hard-drinking heroes or heroines seldom star in today's movies. This may reflect current trends toward more moderate drinking. According to the Institute of Medicine, Americans now drink less distilled beverages than they did in the past.

Some people still do not understand alcoholism. They picture an alcoholic as a bum with dirty, torn clothes, gulping cheap wine from a flask. This false picture of alcoholics perpetuates negative stereotypes. Only 6 percent of the alcoholics in the United States fit this image.[6]

Not everyone in the United States drinks. About one-third of American adults abstain from, do not drink, alcoholic beverages. Some choose not to drink. Some people do not like the taste. Others belong to religions and cultures that restrict alcohol use. According to the American Council on Alcoholism,

40

these restrictions are powerful factors against alcoholism. Muslims, Mormons, Hindus, Christian Scientists, some fundamentalist Christian groups such as Baptists, and strict Jews prohibit alcohol use. Buddhists who practice Zen also do not drink.

Under parental supervision, young people in a family may have small amounts of wine. For some Jewish people, wine is drunk by adults and youth during holiday meals. Catholics drink wine during Mass and at special occasions. Generally, Catholics accept moderate drinking for adults, but drunkenness is a sin.

These cultures and religions generally accept underage drinking, under adult supervision. These young people often grow up with a healthy attitude toward alcohol. As adults, they tend to drink moderately.

The Alcohol Business

Alcohol is big business in the United States. In 1990, U.S. companies produced 8 billion gallons of alcoholic beverages. About 75 percent of that was beer.[7] An American company, E. & J. Gallo Winery in California, is the world's largest wine maker.

The alcohol industry employs over 3.2 million people in the United States, from the alcohol manufacturers to the bartender in the little corner bar. Store, restaurant and tavern owners, distributors, waiters and waitresses, and farmers also profit from alcohol.

The alcohol industry pays more than twenty billion dollars each year in taxes. When people buy a bottle of wine or a six pack of beer, they pay federal taxes. Some states also tax alcohol. The alcohol industry contributes about fifty-two billion dollars to America's economy.[8]

Selling More Alcohol

Although the alcohol beverage industry pays heavy taxes, alcohol is profitable business in America. To increase sales and profits, the industry promotes its products in various ways. American producers of alcoholic beverages spend a lot on marketing studies to find the best ways to sell their products. Alcohol advertising appears in magazines and on television, radio, billboards, posters, buses, and so on. Studies show that alcoholic beverages are the most common drug seen on television.

Some companies use famous spokespeople to sell their products. Others offer free wine samples at liquor stores. Some alcoholic beverages come with attached recipes, to encourage alcohol use in cooking and baking.

Sports is a popular area for alcohol advertising because sports audiences often include many heavy drinkers. Alcohol companies sometimes hire famous athletes for their ads. Most televised athletic events show beer commercials. Breweries also sponsor live athletic events and their ads appear at stadiums or arenas.

In 1991 American alcoholic beverage makers spent more than two billion dollars promoting their products.[9] This breaks down to about 60 percent for beer, 20 percent for wine, and 20 percent for distilled spirits.[10]

Recently the alcohol industry made alcoholic beverages easier to find and buy. Bars and liquor stores stay open longer hours. More liquor stores have opened in neighborhood shopping centers. Lower prices encourage buying. "In many areas, it is possible to buy a 6-pack of beer for less [money] than a 6-pack of some brand-name soft drinks," noted Patricia Taylor, a director at the Center for Science in the Public Interest.[11]

One form of alcohol advertising: a neighborhood bar offers Happy Hour specials. Some organizations want to prohibit Happy Hour because they claim it promotes excessive drinking.

Advertising Ethics

Spokespeople for the alcohol industry claim that their ads only encourage people who already drink to try other brands. However, some question the intent of alcohol ads. Dr. Jean Kilbourne, a former adviser to the U.S. surgeon general, has stated that the three main purposes of advertising are to get new users, increase use among current users, and influence users in their choice among competing brands.

Advertising creates a myth. Ads generally do not educate or give information. Instead, they try to link a product with something people want. Since ads are so common, people tend to accept their messages. Alcohol ads try to promote use among nondrinkers and very light drinkers. They also appeal to the desires and fantasies of a target group that the industry wants to buy its products.

Target groups include those under twenty-one years of age, women, and minority groups. For example, a group of male friends appear on a television ad, all drinking beer in a bar. This ad suggests that if viewers drink this beer, they will be happy and accepted, too. "The beer companies spend hundreds of millions every year to present a very positive image of drinking," said Patricia Taylor.[12]

The Center for Science in the Public Interest, in its book, *The Booze Merchants*, claims that alcohol ads try to persuade nonusers to buy alcohol. Companies spend large amounts of marketing money on young adults and teens. The biggest alcohol consumers are people between the ages of twenty-one and thirty-four. The greatest number of beer drinkers are between the ages of eighteen and twenty-four, although twenty-one is the legal drinking age in this country.[13]

Any business grows by attracting new customers. The

alcohol industry, according to *The Booze Merchants'* authors, is no exception. The authors also claim that many alcohol ads encourage overdrinking. Heavy drinkers consume 50 to 70 percent of all alcoholic beverages sold in the United States.[14]

Many college newspapers and youth-oriented magazines run alcohol ads. Because the minimum drinking age is twenty-one throughout the United States, most readers of these newspapers and magazines cannot legally drink alcohol.

Alcohol accounts for 25 percent of college dropouts. College administrators report that one-third of academic problems can be traced to alcohol use. "Many kids in my senior class are excited about going to college in the fall. They don't care about the classes or learning. They can't wait to party. And partying means drinking," reports one senior high school student.[15]

Alcohol companies use many types of advertising. Alcohol companies sponsor promotions aimed at teens: sports, contests, tasting parties, and rock bands. Critics point out that the average age of rock concert attendees is 15 to 18. Some alcohol companies also sponsor parties and give away beer, T-shirts, posters, and other items with alcohol-brand logos.

Researchers have found that young drinkers take more risks than older drinkers. So, "many alcohol ads feature very risky activities. It is no accident that alcohol companies are leading sponsors of events that appeal to risk-taking and rebellious teenagers: rodeos, ballooning, and racing of motorcycles and dirt bikes, as well as all forms of auto racing."[16]

Some alcoholic-beverage manufacturers try to reach even younger children. In a convenience store's checkout line, a mother watched her nine-year-old daughter try on a free halloween mask. The mask fit. The front of the mask displayed a beer company's large logo.

Few restrictions on alcohol advertising exist. The U.S. Federal Trade Commission (FTC) regulates advertising. It forbids unfair or deceptive advertising. However, it says nothing specific about alcohol advertising.

Some alcohol organizations self-regulate advertising. They follow a code of ethics for advertising standards. The Distilled Spirits Council of the United States, Inc. (DISCUS) publishes a *Code of Good Practice.* The code sets standards for distilled spirits advertisements which include:

- no distilled spirits advertising on television or radio

- discouragement of ads showing teens drinking

- discouragement of ads showing actual drinking or drunkenness.

Advertising Promotes Acceptance

From promotions and ads and by watching television, children and teens learn that drinking is part of everyday life. A 1987 study found that American children between the ages of two and eighteen see about 100,000 beer commercials each year. Under-age drinkers drink about 1.1 billion cans of beer each year. They also consume over one-third of all wine coolers.

Alcohol ads and promotions may or may not increase underage drinking and overuse. One researcher found that "television and movies have the greatest influence on making drugs attractive to children aged 9 to 12 years."[17]

Some American alcohol companies and organizations have started their own alcohol-awareness programs. The Licensed

Beverage Information Council (LBIC), launched in 1979 by ten alcoholic beverage trade organizations, educates people about alcohol abuse. It focuses on four issues: alcohol and pregnancy, drunk driving, treatment of alcoholism, and underage drinking.

The LBIC's teen programs have included funding to support a teen talkline, a telephone referral service for alcohol counseling. The council also developed and distributed a pamphlet for teens that answers the most often-asked questions about alcoholism, and it has produced two educational brochures used in 25,000 classrooms to guide alcohol-use decisions.

However, the selling tactics of alcoholic beverage manufacturers add to confusion about using alcohol wisely. They are sending mixed messages to young people and adults. "I have never seen an alcohol industry program that offers abstinence as a possible choice," stated Dr. Kilbourne.[18]

Laws

Federal, state, and local governments in the United States set the many complex laws regulating alcohol. The federal government regulates alcohol production and the amount of alcohol in a product, some beverage taxes, product labeling, and distribution.

State and local laws regulate alcoholic beverage availability. Laws covering purchase and consumption differ by state, county, and sometimes city by city. State legislatures set the minimum legal age to buy alcohol.

Most state laws allow parents and guardians to serve alcoholic beverages to their children in their own homes. Families may celebrate events and religious holidays by serving alcohol. State laws usually prohibit parents from serving underage youth who are not members of the family.

Who is responsible for the actions of drunk people is a troubling issue. Since the 1800s, most state laws have said public establishments such as bars, taverns, and restaurants and the employed servers of alcohol, such as bartenders, were liable for damages caused by serving alcohol to drunk customers. New laws in over twenty states hold a host or hostess liable for serving alcohol to drunk people if injuries occur. Most of these laws only cover underage drinkers.

Most states have laws that fine or penalize underage youth who try to or do buy alcoholic beverages. People buying alcohol for underage youth, if caught, are also charged and fined. These different rules for adults and underage people exist because children and teens have not yet developed a tolerance to alcohol. They have not learned to compensate for some of its effects and they are still growing and developing. Alcohol affects smaller people more than larger people. Also, teens are learning how to drive a 1,500-pound car. This takes skill, experience, and concentration.

To stop drinking-while-driving, some state laws prohibit open containers of alcoholic beverages in vehicles. States differ in their "Driving While Intoxicated" (DWI) laws, but the accepted blood alcohol level indicating drunkenness is 0.10 percent.

Healthy Lifestyles

Many people today follow healthy lifestyles. Polls show that over two-thirds of Americans want the federal government to inform them of the health hazards of alcohol and discourage overdrinking.

The federal government, however, has contributed little. One reason may be the strong voice of the alcohol industry.

Alcohol is a big, money-making business in the United States. The alcohol lobbying groups (political groups promoting the alcohol industry) in Washington, D.C., are very powerful.

Since 1984, Americans have enjoyed more nonalcoholic and dealcoholized drinks. Nonalcoholic drinks contain no alcohol. They are made from fruits, fruit juices, mineral or carbonated water, and water. Dealcoholized drinks have had their alcohol removed after fermentation or brewing. This leaves the taste, but removes most of the alcohol and calories. Dealcoholized drinks contain about 0.5 percent alcohol. To get the same amount of alcohol that is in one regular glass of beer, a person would have to drink eight glasses of dealcoholized beverages.

Other popular beverages are nutriholic drinks, or drinks that contain fresh fruits, fruit juices, and very small amounts of alcohol. Adults can easily make them at home.

Alcohol affects the appearance and health of those who drink heavily and even of those who drink moderately. The effects differ for each person. Social drinkers can develop broken capillaries. Capillaries are small blood vessels just under the skin. Broken capillaries produce reddish-purple breaks on the skin, especially on the face. Premature wrinkles can also result, because alcohol dehydrates the body. Acne and other skin problems can be traced to moderate drinking. Alcohol puts more blood and so more redness in the face. Over time, damaged skin recovers more slowly from drinking, especially binge drinking.

Hair can lose its shine and become dry and brittle. Eyes can become bloodshot and look smaller because of puffiness. Moderate amounts of alcohol can increase night teeth grinding. It also causes sharp breath odor and stimulates perspiration or sweat odor.

Alcohol is an enemy of weight-watchers. It is high in calories and gives no nutrients to the body. One ounce of liquor contains about 70 calories. That is equal to a fried chicken drumstick. One 12-ounce can of beer has about 150 calories, the same number of calories in a hot dog. Alcohol is the third-leading source of calories in the American diet.[19]

Questions For Discussion

1. Why do you think the American Medical Association changed its definition of alcoholism over the years?

2. Do you think alcohol companies should sponsor events aimed at teens?

3. Do you think alcohol ads should display warnings?

4

Who's an Alcoholic?

Alcoholism and other alcohol problems occur in every group in America. Most alcoholics in the United States are not poor bums. They are working men and women, retired people, and young people. They come from wealthy, middle-class, and poor families.

Children

During the 1940s and 1950s, young people usually had their first drink at age thirteen or fourteen. Today, 30 percent of children have their first drink between the ages of nine and twelve. Recent surveys show that the first drink is typically at age twelve.

Nearly 10 percent of all children have used alcohol by the sixth grade. Others quote higher numbers. The authors of *Loosening the Grip: A Handbook of Alcohol Information* state that, "By age 13, 30% of boys and 22% of girls drink alcohol."[1]

Children also drink more heavily today. A National Council

on Alcoholism and Drug Dependence survey found that 100,000 elementary, school children get drunk at least once a week.

Children say that peer pressure, pressure from friends, is the most common reason to try alcohol. A 1990 survey found that over one-third of fourth graders said they feel pressure to drink. By sixth grade, the rate rose to 50 percent.

Alcohol misinformation could also be a factor. A recent survey of fourth, fifth, and sixth graders found that only 21 percent said wine coolers are a drug, but half of them listed alcohol as a drug.

Teens

Teen alcohol use remains at high levels. In a 1991 Gallup International Institute survey, 80 percent of high school sports coaches said alcohol is a "very" or "somewhat big" problem among teens. A recent poll by the National Association of Student Councils found that "alcohol was the leading school problem and 46 percent [of students] said it was the school's most serious problem."[2]

Of the 20.7 million teens in the United States:

- 300,000 are alcoholics. Another 4.6 million are problem drinkers.

- At least 454,000 binge drink once a week. Binge drinkers gulp 5 or more drinks in an hour. About 40 percent of college students binge drink regularly.

- 10 to 20 percent say drinking is a major problem for them.

- 8 million drink weekly.

- One out of four teens gets drunk at least four times a year.

Why do teens drink? "I'll ask kids in treatment to raise their hands [to show] how many used because of peer pressure, family or school problems, or just because it was fun," said a director of a treatment center for youth and families. "They laugh because they raise their hands for all these reasons."[3]

In a recent national survey, about 25 percent of teens said they drink to get drunk; they do not care about the taste. Another 25 percent drink because they are bored. Peer pressure is another major factor. Teens want approval and acceptance from peers. So, when other teens push them to drink, some do.

Some shy teens drink to help loosen up, to fit into a crowd, or to gain courage and ask for a date. Others drink to numb pain, fear, despair, or depression. About 41 percent of teens drink to help them cope with their feelings.

Some teens imitate the adults around them who drink. They view drinking as being adult. Some boast of how much alcohol they drink in a night. Others drink to defy or rebel against adult rules. Still other teens use alcohol out of curiosity.

"Kids at my senior high school drink, not because they enjoy it, but because they think it's cool. It's status to say, 'Hey, I got drunk last night.' They do it for popularity and because they think other kids will respect them. I think a lot of these kids drink because of low self-esteem," explained Jake Trippel, a high school senior in White Bear Lake, Minnesota.

"Kids go to parties to get drunk. Out of my senior class of 556 kids, I'd say a third to a half get drunk at weekly parties.

The typical alcoholic American

Doctor, age 54

Farmer, age 35

Unemployed, age 40

College student, age 19

Counselor, age 38

Retired editor, age 86

Dancer, age 22

Police officer, age 46

Military officer, age 31

Student, age 14

Executive, age 50

Taxi driver, age 61

Homemaker, age 43

Bricklayer, age 29

Computer programmer, age 25

Lawyer, age 52

There's no such thing as typical. We have all kinds.
10 million Americans are alcoholic.
It's our number one drug problem.

For information or help, contact
National Clearinghouse for Alcohol and Drug Information, P.O. Box 2345, Rockville, MD 20852
1-800-729-6686

U.S. DEPARTMENT OF HEALTH AND HUMAN SERVICES • Public Health Service • Alcohol, Drug Abuse, and Mental Health Administration
Prepared and published by the Office for Substance Abuse Prevention

DHHS Publication No. (ADM) 91-1901

The disease of alcoholism can develop in all kinds of people.

They have stupid contests at these parties. One I heard about is called Quarters. Eight to ten kids sit around a table. They take a quarter, call heads or tails, and then flip it. Losers put a shot of whatever alcohol they are drinking into a big glass that sits in the middle of the table. At the end of the game, the loser drinks down the whole big glass. The loser usually gets pretty sick."

Jake continued, "Kids are scared of using cocaine and crack. They know these drugs can kill them. They think alcohol won't hurt them. They don't think of or know about the long-term effects of alcohol. I don't drink or do drugs. After badly injuring my knee playing basketball, I now train and weight lift to take care of my body."[4]

Keith Schooler, twenty-seven, went to high school in Indianapolis, Indiana. He remembers, "During our junior and senior years, the thing to do on weekends was to party. Most weekends, a group of four or five of us close friends would get together at someone's house. We'd party to get drunk. Sometimes, when parents were out of town, we'd have larger parties of twenty to thirty kids. The object of these parties was to drink as much as possible. It was cool to say 'I got smashed this weekend.'"

"You know, when I look back, it was all pretty stupid." Keith shook his head. "I'd get smashed Friday nights. Then I'd get up with a horrible hangover, feeling really sick, and go to work at my Saturday job. That night, I'd get smashed again. Sunday would be a waste because I'd feel so sick."[5]

A lack of knowledge about alcohol contributes toward teen drinking. A federal survey found that one-third of all teens did not understand the effects of alcohol. For example, many teens did not know that someone could die from an alcohol overdose.

GOVERNMENT WARNING:
(1) ACCORDING TO THE SURGEON GENERAL,
WOMEN SHOULD NOT DRINK ALCOHOLIC BEVERAGES
DURING PREGNANCY BECAUSE OF THE RISK OF BIRTH DEFECTS.
(2) CONSUMPTION OF ALCOHOLIC BEVERAGES IMPAIRS YOUR
ABILITY TO DRIVE A CAR OR OPERATE MACHINERY, AND MAY
CAUSE HEALTH PROBLEMS.

WATER, FORTIFIED WHITE WINE, HIGH FRUCTOSE
CORN SYRUP, NATURAL FLAVORS, TARTARIC ACID,
TRISODIUM CITRATE, CITRIC ACID, CARAMEL COLOR
POTASSIUM SORBATE AND SULFUR DIOXIDE

TROPICAL FLAVORED WINE COOLER,
ALC 5% BY VOL, 12FL OZ - 355 ML

BREWED TO HIGHEST QUALITY STANDARDS WITH PURE
WATER, CHOICEST HOPS, FINEST BARLEY MALT, CORN
AND CULTURED YEAST

All of these labels describe alcoholic beverages. Look for these words:
alcohol, alc., malt beer, brewed, malt ale, wine. Also, by law, any
alcoholic beverage must have a label warning of the effects of alcohol.

About 25 percent did not know the minimum legal age to buy alcohol in every state is twenty-one.

A recent national survey for the government found that two-thirds of teens cannot tell alcoholic beverages from nonalcoholic beverages. Many did not know that wine coolers contain alcohol. They also confused wine coolers with mineral waters. Wine coolers are often similar in color, labeling, and packaging. Some coolers are not clearly labeled as alcoholic.

In most states, beer and other malt beverages do not display their alcohol content on labels. So teens cannot tell how much alcohol the beverages contain. Federal law prohibits beer and malt liquor beverage companies from putting alcohol content on labels. This law went into effect after Prohibition was repealed in 1933 to prevent companies from using alcohol content to attract drinkers.

Another factor in teen drinking is that alcohol is often easy to get. Many parents keep some at home. A recent federal study found that of the almost 7 million teens who drink, about two-thirds buy their own alcohol. Teens also get alcohol from friends. Jake Trippel agrees. "Kids at my school usually have someone older buy them alcohol. A lot of kids know someone who's twenty-one or older. Some have brothers and sisters over twenty-one. Because most seniors in my high school have jobs, money to buy alcohol is no problem."[6]

Teens tend to drink more than adults. Also, teens get drunk more easily, usually because they are smaller and less experienced drinkers than adults.

Surveys show that no differences in rates of drinking exist between teens from wealthy, middle, or lower-class families. Nondrinking rates are highest among African-American and

VANESSA WAS IN A FATAL CAR ACCIDENT LAST NIGHT. ONLY SHE DOESN'T KNOW IT YET.

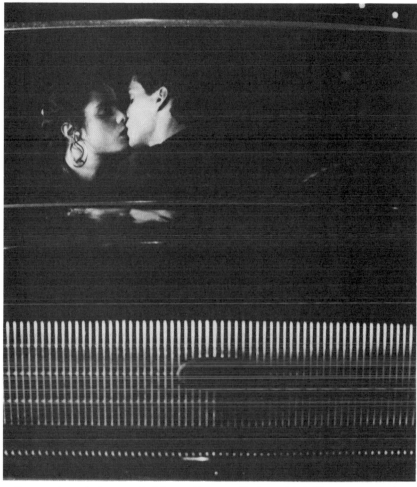

Every year, thousands of young people die in car accidents caused by drugs and alcohol. But now you can wreck your life without hitting the gas pedal. The number of reported AIDS cases among teenagers has increased by 96% in the last two years. If you get high and forget, even for a moment, how risky sex can be, you're putting your life on the line. Call 1-800-662-HELP for help and information. **AIDS. ANOTHER WAY DRUGS CAN KILL.**

Teens who drink are more likely to have unprotected sex. This increases their chances of getting or passing AIDS.

Asian-American teens. The highest teen drinking rates are among white and Native-American male and female high school seniors and Mexican-American males. These groups are also statistically among the heaviest drinkers.

Alcohol is a factor with teens who were involved in crime, suicide, pregnancy, auto accidents, and hospital admissions. A Massachusetts study of sixteen- to nineteen-year-olds who drink found that 49 percent were more likely to have sex if both partners had been drinking. Sexually active teens who drink are more likely to have unprotected sex. This increases their exposure to AIDS.

Teens often do not know when they have alcohol problems. Usually, parents, teachers, counselors, or adult friends spot the problem, based on the teen's behavior. Problem teen drinkers may let their grades slide, get caught stealing, get arrested, cause accidents, or perform poorly at after-school jobs.

Most teens who use illegal drugs first used alcohol. Usually, they continue to use alcohol along with other drugs. But, the American Council on Alcoholism has stated that alcohol is not a gateway drug, and that alcohol does not lead teens to hard drug addiction. "This type of myth is a 'scare tactic' to make young people fear alcoholic beverages."[7] Most teens do not become alcoholics and drug addicts.

Women

One-third of all American women are alcoholics. This is a total of about five million. Some researchers estimate half of all alcoholics are women.

Chronic alcohol abuse takes a greater physical toll on women than men. Women are more likely to develop liver disease than men. A 1992 study found that women alcoholics have death rates 50 to 100 percent higher than male alcoholics and lose fifteen years from their lives because of cirrhosis, heart problems, suicide, murder, and alcohol-related accidents.

Alcohol tends to affect women differently than men. Women are usually smaller and have more body fat than men. They have less water in their bodies to dilute alcohol. So they generally get drunk faster. Women also tend to break down alcohol more slowly than men. Alcohol interferes with calcium absorption. Women who are heavy drinkers may find their bones becoming softer and more brittle. This increases their risk of bone damage.

Some women use alcohol to cope with personal problems. Handling a job and children and running a household can be stressful. Some women cannot cope when adult children move away from home. Women are more likely than men to combine alcohol with medicines. Since alcohol does not mix with over one hundred medicines, results can be serious. Women are also more likely than men to drink secretly, often at home.

The Elderly

Alcohol abuse for those over sixty-five is a serious problem. About 2 to 10 percent or 0.8 to 4 million elderly people abuse alcohol. Other researchers estimate that 20 percent of the elderly abuse alcohol.

Some elderly people have been alcoholics for many years. Others become alcoholics later in life. They may use alcohol to help cope with personal problems: retirement, poor health, or death of a loved one or a friend.

One grave danger of alcoholism in the elderly is that it can mask chest pain. This pain could be a heart attack warning.

Alcoholism can also produce symptoms similar to other illnesses, including confusion and memory lapses. If a doctor is unaware of alcohol abuse, the wrong diagnosis and treatment could result.

Another danger is alcohol and drug interactions. The 40 million elderly take 25 percent of all prescribed medicines. Nearly half of them have serious diseases such as arthritis, diabetes, heart disease, or lung disease. The elderly also use a lot of over-the-counter drugs.

Ethnic Groups

Researchers have reported on various American ethnic groups and their drinking trends. One trend stands out: Whites drink more, as a group, than any other American ethnic group. Here are other trends.

African Americans. More African Americans abstain from alcohol than white people. Nearly half of African-American women abstain. Overall, African-American teens and young adults drink less than white teens. Heavy drinking among African-American males increases after age 30 and remains high through old age. African-American males are at very high risk for alcohol-related diseases.

Hispanics. Alcoholism, especially among men, is strongly denied by Hispanic Americans. Many agree that "getting drunk is an innocent way to have fun" and wait until weekends to drink heavily.[8] Nearly 70 percent of Hispanic men drink. Of these, 36 percent drink heavily. About half of Hispanic women abstain.

Native Americans. In 1991 alcohol abuse rates among some Native-American groups were twice that of whites. Other groups are almost all abstainers. Binge drinking is common in those groups who drink. Alcohol is involved in 75 percent of

Native American traumatic deaths, such as suicide or traffic crashes. A 1989 Minnesota survey found that Native-American teens had higher rates than white teens on alcohol problem drinking, such as binge drinking. Economic stress and family instability are factors in these drinking rates.

Recent surveys show good news, however. Alcohol use rates by Native Americans are dropping. The U.S. Health Service projects that by 2005, Native American alcohol rates will reduce to the rates among whites. Treatment at earlier ages is helping. So is increased cultural awareness, especially among teens.

Others. Asian Americans have low levels of alcohol abuse. Alcohol abuse among the homeless is high, from 20 to 45 percent. Sometimes this leads to frostbite and gangrene. Alcoholic homeless people are also more likely to get tuberculosis.

Worldwide Alcohol Use

Alcohol is produced by all countries worldwide except strict Islamic states, such as Saudi Arabia. Alcohol is consumed in most countries, too.

Alcohol drinking in Europe is decreasing but is still fairly high. Many Italians drink wine with meals. About 9 percent of Italians are alcoholics, and nearly 200,000 die each year from cirrhosis.[9] Police there seldom test for drunk driving. A sociology professor at the University of Turin, Italy, believes that "Italy has had alcohol problems a long time, but always hidden."[10]

France's rate of heavy drinking is the world's highest. French children learn to drink wine early and often. France has a high rate of alcohol-related problems. Its cirrhosis death rate is twice that of the United States.

Public drunkenness in Finland is common. Drunken driving, however, is not. Special police often spot-check drivers. About 17 percent, or 100 each year, of Finland's traffic deaths are alcohol-related. In comparison, in the United States, about half of the 45,000 highway deaths each year are alcohol related.[11]

South Koreans now consume more distilled spirits than any other nation. Business meetings often include drinking. Another Asian nation, Japan, also has high drinking rates. Today, the Japanese drink twice what they did in 1950. Drinking after work is almost company policy at many businesses. On the streets of Japan, vending machines sell cans of beer or Scotch and soda.

However, half of all Asians have an altered gene or mutation. (A mutation is a change in a gene that can be inherited.) Asian people with this mutation cannot completely break down alcohol, and this causes them to get very sick if they drink. Their faces may flush. They may sweat a lot and vomit.

In the former Soviet Union, drinking is part of its past and modern people. Some people, including former Soviet leader Leonid Brezhnev, have declared vodka the national drink. Alcoholism in the former Soviet Union is estimated at over 20 million people. Alcohol costs 1 million Russian lives and more than $300 billion each year.

From 1985 to 1987, Mikhail Gorbachev, a former Soviet leader, tried to stop his people from drinking. He closed all bars, beer, and distilled spirits plants. The rate of alcohol poisoning, which killed 40,000 Russians each year, dropped. But people continued to drink. They made their own alcohol or drank things with alcohol in them, such as shoe polish and cologne.

Controls have eased, but today few bars are open. Buying wine at a store can take three to four hours of standing in line.

"We still have great shortages," said one Russian citizen. "But when you see a line in front of a grocery store, you know they have vodka."[12]

Despite problems buying alcohol, people still drink. Dr. David Musto, Yale University School of Medicine, estimated that, "Today the average family here [in the former Soviet Union] spends about one-fifth its income on alcohol, compared to less than one-twenty-fifth in the United States."[13] Every night, the national alcohol police gathers drunken people off Moscow's streets.

Questions For Discussion

1. Why do you think drinking has become company policy for many Japanese businesses?

2. Since so many teens drink, do you think the legal drinking age of twenty-one should be lowered? Why or why not?

3. Both America and the former Soviet Union tried to stop alcohol use by outlawing its sale. Both countries reversed their laws. Based on these experiments, should the United States legalize narcotics? Why or why not?

5

Families and Alcohol?

Alcohol abuse often creates great pain in families. About 25 percent, or one in four, American homes have been hurt by an alcohol-related family problem. Seven million teens and children live in alcoholic homes. About 3 million of these young people will eventually become alcoholics, develop other drug problems, or have serious coping problems.[1]

People have long recognized that alcoholism tends to run in families. "Bill [Wilson] had been warned since childhood not to touch alcohol. His mother had divorced his father largely because of drink. . . . If Bill once began, he had been warned, he, too, might get into trouble."[2] After Bill Wilson became a recovering alcoholic, he cofounded Alcoholics Anonymous in 1935.

Why this family connection persists has fueled many debates among researchers. Studies show that someone is more likely to become an alcoholic if a close or blood relative is an alcoholic.

However, these studies do not prove that alcoholism is inherited. Current research suggests that both genetics and environment, or the home life, are factors.

Genetics or Environment?

Twin and adoption studies support the idea that genetics, heredity, causes alcoholism. An early study of alcoholism in twins found that if one identical twin was an alcoholic, the chance the other twin was also an alcoholic was 74 percent.

In a large 1987 study, researchers examined more than 2,800 pairs of twins. They concluded that genetics play an important role in drinking patterns.

In adoption studies, researchers study genetics and home life independently. A special report to the U.S. Congress examined many adoption studies. The report's conclusion: Adopted children born to alcoholic parents are at greater risk for alcoholism than adopted children born to nonalcoholics.

Of the 100,000 genes in each person, researchers have not discovered one gene that determines if someone will become an alcoholic. Instead, some researchers suggest that a group of genes must be present. Others search for biological markers, such as specific brain wave changes. Scientists could use biological markers to identify specific genes.

Recently, a neuroscientist at State University of New York College of Medicine in Brooklyn, New York, found a brain wave marker in sons of alcoholics. Based on his work, he believes that some people tend to become alcoholics because of their genes. He explained, "Alcoholism is different from Huntington's disease, a directly inherited disease caused by a single gene—you have the gene, you get Huntington's. What you inherit in alcoholism is not a disease, it's a predisposition."[3]

Some scientists say that the family environment is the main factor in the development of alcoholism. If teens see one or both parents drink heavily, they will imitate what they see. They will learn to abuse alcohol. Or, they may not want to drink when they see alcoholism's devastation.

Researchers find that the family is very important in setting alcohol standards. Parents who drink a small amount with meals and who are consistent in their behaviors set a healthy example for teens. Also, if parents do not use alcohol as the main focus of an activity or to cope with problems, then teens learn positive alcohol use.

Researchers agree that a history of alcohol abuse in a family signals that a teen is at higher risk of becoming an alcoholic. Many also agree that no single cause of alcoholism exists.

A Family Disease

"Alcoholism is a family disease," said a director of a family therapy clinic. "Alcoholism can kill the alcoholic. But it's the behavior that does all the other damage."[4] An alcoholic impacts the entire family. Family members cannot escape or ignore the alcoholic.

Because of their strong emotional ties, family members are deeply affected by the alcoholic. Alcoholism seals off the alcoholic from other people. It also isolates family members from each other. The family's world shrinks to guard the alcoholic's drinking. Each family member is affected differently by the alcoholic, because people react to stress in different ways.

69

Family members often have many negative feelings. They may feel suspicious, insecure, disappointed, fearful, isolated, guilty, or embarrassed. They resent the alcoholic but often cover up all their negative feelings.[5]

Alcohol use contributes to violence at home. Researchers report that:

- 52 percent of all spouse abusers have a history of alcoholism.

- 38 percent of child abusers have problems with alcohol.

- 65 percent of all child abuse is alcohol-related.

Children of Alcoholics

Researchers began studying children of alcoholics (COAs) in the 1970s. Today, researchers estimate that 28.6 million Americans have or had at least one alcoholic parent. This figure includes almost 7 million children and teens. So, in a classroom of twenty-five students, four to six may be COAs.

Researchers have learned that COAs are at greater risk to become alcoholics than people who are not COAs. Sons of alcoholics are four times more likely, and daughters are three times more likely. Also, COAs are four times more likely to marry an alcoholic and re-create the same stressful families they grew up in; and COAs, especially older teens, are at increased risk for other drug use. However, most COAs do not become alcoholics.

The National Institute on Alcohol Abuse and Alcoholism estimates that more than 40 percent of COAs do develop serious problems in coping, or ways of handling problems or stress.

Alcoholism in the family shapes children's and teens' attitudes and their personalities. COAs generally have a hard time knowing what is real and what is not. This is because in an alcoholic family, reality is denied.

For example, drinking, fighting, and abuse can flare one night. The next day, parents act as though nothing happened. Or a teen may talk with a drunken parent one evening. When the teen refers to the talk the next day, the parent may not remember. The parent probably suffered a blackout and has no memory of a drinking episode. Some COAs will not bring friends to their homes because of an alcoholic parent's possible behaviors.

COAs often try to make things easier for or to help the alcoholic. They might lie or cover for him or her. Or they might hide or dump bottles of alcohol or replace some alcohol with water. By repeating these actions, over time, COAs stop listening to their own feelings and instincts.

They also learn not to trust their parents and to never talk about family problems with others. Claudia Black, a leading researcher on children of alcoholics, described the often unspoken rules in alcoholic families: "Don't talk, don't trust, don't feel."[6]

Teens do not know when chaos will erupt in their alcoholic homes. Their homes are filled with conflict, tension, and stress. As a result, many COAs feel depressed and anxious. Children may be afraid to go to school, wet their beds, cry, or have nightmares. Teen COAs may try to be perfect, hoard things, isolate themselves, or develop fears. They also sometimes have school problems. They cut classes, drop out of school, or repeat grades. Often COAs think they are failures, even if they earn good grades.[7]

Some common traits of COAs include:

- Fear of losing control.

- Inability to remember large portions of childhood years.

- Poor stress management.

- Addiction to excitement, drugs, gambling, or overeating.

- Feelings of isolation, abandonment, or depression.

- Denial of problems.[8]

COA Roles in the Family

In alcoholic families, COAs often take on one of four roles. These roles help children and teens survive unstable homes. The following definitions of the roles are not rigid but are guides to help understand COA behaviors. The four COA roles are the hero or superachiever, the scapegoat or rebel, the lost child, and the mascot.

The hero or superachiever is usually the oldest child. Heroes try to be perfect. They earn good school grades and keep the family going, especially in a crisis. They blame themselves if parents continue to drink.

The scapegoat or rebel is often the second child. Scapegoats take the blame for family problems. They often do poorly in school and sometimes take drugs, steal, or end up in jail. Because the family focuses on dealing with the problem child, they do not have the time or energy to deal with the alcoholic.

The lost child tends to be the middle child. Lost children stay in the background and seldom get into trouble. They spend a lot of time alone in their rooms.

All family members like the mascot. Mascots are cute and fun. They divert or diffuse the family from a crisis with jokes or clowning. Mascots use humor to ease tense moments.

COAs sometimes move from one role to another, depending on the situation. If the oldest child, a hero, moves away to college, another child may jump into the hero role. This child will learn to cook, shop, clean, and manage the household. The hero and scapegoat roles most often interchange in alcoholic families.

Adult COAs

Parents can also be COAs. If their parents drank too much, they may have grown up in an alcoholic home. Some adult COAs may:

- be afraid of close friendships and relationships. They find it hard to trust others, even their own mates or children.

- be uncomfortable with authority. This includes older people, people in uniform, doctors, nurses, employers, and so on.

- try to control others. Sometimes they smother their children and overprotect them.

- work hard to give their children a better life than they had. However, they may feel jealous of their children for having more material things.[9]

Help for Families

Alcoholics need help, and so do their families. Family members can learn to free themselves from the effects of the alcoholic on their lives. First, though, nonalcoholic members must learn to change their attitudes, then their behaviors. They need to learn about alcoholism, understand family behaviors, and get help from outside the family.

Learning about alcoholism helps the family understand how to deal with this disease. For example, many people would say these statements are true. However, they are **all** false:

- If people drink only beer or wine, they cannot get drunk.

- It is easy to spot an alcoholic.

- People who drink only on weekends cannot be alcoholics.

The family loves and cares about the alcoholic, but they tend to react to the alcoholic's behavior. Their thinking and behaviors center on dealing with the alcoholic. They often neglect their own needs. By getting help, family members can begin to understand their own problems and also the family's problems.

Once family members see their own distorted behaviors, they can learn how to change. Therapists say that the hardest step in healing is for the child or teen to talk about negative feelings. Many COAs try to keep the alcoholic's drinking a secret. They often ignore and try to defend their actions and those of the alcoholic.

Once family members begin to talk and heal, they can then focus on themselves and their needs, care for others, and trust their own feelings. They also learn that no matter how hard their problems, help is available and, most importantly, that they control their own lives.

COAs learn to cope with their family situations in healthy ways, even if the alcoholic continues to drink. For example, some COAs get involved with clubs, teams, hobbies, and fun activities at school.

To figure out needs and learn new behaviors, teens can turn to different resources for help. Professional counselors or therapists offer individual, family, or group therapy. Other possible resources include a teacher, counselor, coach, clergy, family friend, social worker, or relative. Peers are also excellent support. Three national peer self-help organizations are Alateen, Al-Anon, and the National Association for Children of Alcoholics.

Alateen is a free support organization for teens affected by someone else's drinking. The drinker can be a family member or a friend. Alateen, part of Al-Anon Family Groups, started in 1957. Today, Alateen includes 4,100 groups worldwide, with over 45,000 members.

Each Alateen group has a sponsor, who usually is an active Al-Anon member. New members usually receive extra support. At each Alateen meeting, table cards remind members that,

Who you see here
What you hear here
When you leave here
Let it stay here

10. Al-Anon Family Group Headquarters, Meeting Table Card, undated.

IS ALCOHOL A PROBLEM IN YOUR FAMILY?

ALATEEN
**HELP FOR TEENAGERS WHOSE PARENT, RELATIVE OR FRIEND
IS A PROBLEM DRINKER**

CALL: (   )   IN:

3-10M-90 - 5/1.00   OR CONTACT 1-800-356-9996   AL-ANON FAMILY GROUP HEADQUARTERS, P.O. BOX 862, MIDTOWN STATION, NEW YORK, N.Y. 10018-0862   M-41s

Alateen offers teens support if alcoholism is a problem in their family, or if a close friend or relative is having problems with alcohol.

This anonymity and confidentiality of Alateen members ensures a safe place to grow and relate to others with similar experiences. No formats exist for Alateen meetings, but most center on a theme. Members share their experiences, problems, and coping ideas around the theme. They learn protective skills, including how to deal with a drunk parent. They also learn that they did not cause someone to drink and that they cannot stop someone from drinking.

Al-Anon started in 1951 as a spinoff from Alcoholics Anonymous (AA). This free resource is a mutual support system for anyone affected by someone else's alcoholism. It provides information and help for families and friends, even if the alcoholic does not seek help. As of 1992, Al-Anon groups meet in 104 countries worldwide and include over half a million members. Members talk about their experiences and give emotional support to each other.

Al-Anon Family Groups, headquartered in New York, includes both Al-Anon and Alateen. Their publications are available in twenty-nine languages, as well as in Braille and on tape. Where no groups exist, Al-Anon provides a Lone Member Service. Al-Anon meetings have been held in prisons, hospitals, and other nontraditional places.

The Children of Alcoholics (COAs) movement started in the early 1980s. Organizers wanted help with problems associated with growing up in an alcoholic family. In 1983, the National Association for Children of Alcoholics (NACoA) formed. NACoA strives to "support and serve as a resource for COAs of all ages and those in a position to help them."[11] Among its services, NACoA distributes a list of self-help groups for COAs.

Questions For Discussion

1. Geneticists hope to develop a test to determine genetic predisposition to alcohol use. Can you see any potential conflicts in the use of such a test?

2. Because of their family alcoholism, many teen COAs find it difficult to develop friendships. Suggest some ways teens can learn to trust one another.

3. Sometimes it is hard for teens to ask for help. Suggest some ways teens can ask for the help they need.

6

Treatment and Prevention

Few Treatment Choices

Before the 1940s, alcoholics in the United States had few treatment choices. The typical way to deal with problem drinkers was to jail them. Once sober, they were released. Because these people received no medical or treatment help, many cycled in and out of jail.

Lois Wilson, the wife of the cofounder of Alcoholics Anonymous wrote, "[In 1945] facilities for detoxification were rare everywhere. Doctors considered alcoholic patients a nuisance, unreliable in paying and morally weak. Few physicians took them seriously or had the patience to treat them. Most hospitals refused to admit them."[1]

Today, many types of treatment exist for problem drinkers. Treatments depend on the type of alcoholism. No one has found a cure for this disease, but alcoholism can be controlled.

Each year about 1.5 million Americans seek alcoholism treatment, at a total cost of $15 billion each year. Many recover and lead happy and satisfying lives. Others do not recover. Still other alcoholics who could be helped never seek treatment. However, the federal government reports that alcoholism treatment services and numbers of people in treatment are increasing.

Alcoholics Anonymous

Alcoholics Anonymous (AA) has helped thousands recover from alcoholism. It is the oldest treatment program and was started by two alcoholics in 1935. In 1939 AA could count only one hundred sober members. After national magazines published articles about AA, membership grew to 100,000 in 1950. Today, membership exceeds two million worldwide; AA membership in the United States alone exceeds one million.

Alcoholics Anonymous still retains its original goal: to be a self-help group for those who want to stop drinking and stay sober. Its members follow a series of twelve steps. These steps help alcoholics admit they have a drinking problem and then help them change their behaviors. The steps also offer guidelines to help members cope with future problems. The organization publishes many materials and some especially for teens.

Anyone who has or had a drinking problem can attend AA meetings, even if they are not in other treatment programs. No one pays dues or fees. No one records the meetings, which last from sixty to ninety minutes. In large cities, AA offers groups for teens, women, men, various language groups, and gays and lesbians. Different types of meetings are held:

- Beginner meetings for newcomers focus on tools to stop drinking, such as what to do at a party.

- Step meetings focus on one of the twelve steps and how to use it in daily living.

- General open meetings for all members.

Treatment for Teen Alcoholics

Today, five treatment programs exist to help teen alcoholics.

Crisis intervention services are usually in hospitals. They treat teens and others with a serious or overdose reaction to alcohol or other drugs. Most teens do not need crisis intervention services. If they do, they usually stay between a few days and several weeks. After treatment, counseling is available, and teens are usually referred to other types of treatment.

Inpatient hospital programs provide both psychological and medical services. Often, teens go through individual, group, and family counseling. They learn new behaviors to help them cope with their regular lives. Inpatient programs are usually brief, lasting about two months.

Residential treatment programs, or halfway houses, remove teens from their homes and schools and move them to a new location, away from the temptation of alcohol. If teens are a danger to themselves or to others, they are usually put into these programs. Here, teens learn about themselves, the consequences of their drunken actions, and why and how to stop drinking and stay sober. Typical residential programs run from two to twelve months. Teens may be involved in individual and group counseling, self-help groups, educational activities, and drug education. Many programs include outdoor or wilderness

Many alcoholics never seek treatment, although many treatment options are available.

activities. These help teens develop self-esteem and trust in others.

Day treatment programs provide teens treatment four-plus hours a day, between five and seven days a week. Teens go to school, then to the day treatment program, and return home at night. These programs offer individual counseling, self-help teen groups, group and family counseling, and referral to other types of treatment. They also offer a variety of educational services so teens can keep up in school. Fun time is planned for teens to swim or play volleyball, for example. These programs last from two to twenty four months.

Clinic programs provide a wide range of services, from drop-in centers to structured activities. Day treatment services are often available in a clinic program but are less intense. Community mental health centers, YMCAs, YWCAs, and private businesses usually provide clinic programs. Teens attend one or more times a week, for one to three hours per session. Programs run from two to twenty-four months.

Other Treatment for Alcoholism

Some people recover and stop depending on alcohol by attending AA meetings. Others require a different treatment type or a variety of treatments.

In the United States, alcohol treatment programs focus on three phases:

- detoxing (detoxifying) or managing alcohol withdrawal

- recovery or long-term management of alcohol dependence

- preventing drinking again

A detoxification (detox) center provides a safe place to withdraw from alcohol. All alcoholics go through withdrawal. However, most do not go to a detox center.

Alcohol withdrawal differs for each person. People may become restless, sweat, shake, or hallucinate. A craving for alcohol is common. Some people become delirious or cannot sleep. Alcohol withdrawal, ridding the body of alcohol, usually lasts five days but can take several weeks.

Trained personnel help alcoholics through withdrawal. They evaluate alcoholics for medical and psychological problems. Sometimes doctors give medicines to help alcoholics through withdrawal. Because the craving for alcohol is strong during withdrawal, some prescribe a drug called Antabuse.

Antabuse discourages alcoholics from returning to alcohol. By itself, Antabuse produces no reactions. Once alcoholics drink, though, even a small amount of alcohol will trigger cramps, nausea, headaches, and dizziness. The reactions are swift and severe. Not all people want to take Antabuse, and doctors do not prescribe it too often.

Sometimes, alcoholics who withdraw from alcohol take tranquilizers. Tranquilizers are drugs that doctors use to calm people and to reduce their stress. However, they do not help alcoholics who are withdrawing from alcohol. Sometimes alcoholics become addicted to tranquilizers instead of alcohol. Also, because both tranquilizers and alcohol are depressants, by mixing the two, alcoholics could become very ill. That is because the effects of both drugs together are stronger than if each drug was taken alone.

84

Through posters like this one, people are more aware of the growing problem of teen alcoholism — and that many treatment choices are available.

After withdrawal, alcoholics often go to a recovery program, such as an in-hospital treatment program, outpatient hospital program, or residential or day treatment programs. These programs are important, because if teens or others go home right after detox, they usually start drinking again. That is because they have not learned other ways to deal with their lives, other than by drinking. Detox can also occur at any recovery program.

In most recovery programs, teens and other alcoholics are closely supervised. They go through individual and group counseling, alcohol education classes, and AA meetings. Teens also learn communication skills, how to be assertive, and how to resist peer pressure.

Families are an important part of teen treatment because alcoholism is usually a family problem. Many programs include family therapy once a week. Family members are referred to self-help groups such as Al-Anon, Alateen, and Families Anonymous.

Treatment costs vary and depend on the type of treatment, whether it is public or private treatment, and the severity of the alcohol abuse. Six months of treatment can cost from $1,000 to $10,000.

Despite treatment, alcoholics are not cured. They have a lifelong disease that they can learn to control. Usually, once treated, alcoholics cannot have another drink without the symptoms of alcoholism reoccurring. So, these alcoholics call themselves recovering or nondrinking alcoholics.

Once alcoholics return to their homes, schools, jobs, and communities, they need emotional support and acceptance. Although the alcoholic has stopped drinking, life and all its

86

problems continue. Recovering alcoholics generally face a variety of problems such as:

- low self-esteem and self-acceptance

- life-style changes

- how to deal with saying no to drinking

- whether to tell others that they're recovering alcoholics

- changes in family and friends

Treatment programs recommend that recovering alcoholics attend AA meetings two or three times a week because AA offers alcoholics emotional support. Studies show that those who attend AA after treatment are more likely to remain sober than those who do not attend. Family members are also encouraged to go to regular Al-Anon or Alateen meetings.

Many alcoholics have at least one relapse, a period of time when they drink again, within a year or two after treatment. This does not mean that the person or treatment failed. Most people who relapse do not start drinking heavily again. After additional treatment, many never drink again. Why relapses happen is unclear, although researchers are studying this problem.

Some people find that AA does not give them enough long-term emotional support. For example, one former nurse, a recovering alcoholic, said that AA did not feel right for her. "I didn't like the intense religious focus, and talking about my past just made me want to drink."[2]

As a result, other alternative self-help groups have sprung up over the past twenty years. Unlike AA, the newer programs do not talk about God or a higher power. Instead, they emphasize the personal strengths within each person. Three of the largest alternative groups to help alcoholics stay sober are Rational Recovery, Secular Organization for Sobriety, and Women for Sobriety.

Rational Recovery (RR) Founded in 1986, RR now has chapters in most states as well as worldwide. At least 10,000 people have gone through RR. This program teaches people to recognize their addictive traits and how to develop coping skills or change behavior.

Up to fourteen people form each RR group. Unlike AA, each group has a professional adviser, such as a medical doctor, psychologist, social worker, or nurse. Founder Jack Trimpey encourages members to graduate from their RR groups within one year.

Secular Organization for Sobriety (SOS) James Christopher, a former alcoholic, founded SOS in 1986. This worldwide program now has over 20,000 members and encourages alcoholics to deal with their alcoholism one day at a time.

Groups average about twenty people. Each group member takes turns as the moderator. Meetings are not structured and consist of general discussions about members' issues. Some members go to weekly meetings. Others go every few months or twice a year.

Women for Sobriety (WFS) This group is the first national self-help program for women alcoholics. Jean Kirkpatrick, a recovering alcoholic, founded WFS in 1975. Today, WFS has about 5,000 members worldwide.

The organization emphasizes self-esteem and self-strength.

Members follow thirteen positive statements. Women give each other emotional support for daily living. Unlike AA, the women do not spend much time discussing alcoholism and their past. Instead, they focus on their present lives or their future. Meetings are limited to ten women and are held once a week. Some members go every few months or years.

New Alcoholism Treatment Methods

The federal government, through the National Institute on Alcohol Abuse and Alcoholism (NIAAA), provides over $25 million each year for researchers to develop new and better treatment methods. No single treatment method works for all people with alcohol problems. With NIAAA support, researchers have recently developed new tools to help health professionals assess teens' alcoholism, and determine what treatments might work best.

The institute sponsors many large studies about alcoholism treatment. Some of these studies help to:

- determine which treatments best prevent relapses.

- find what treatments work best for women and the homeless.

- learn if medicines, such as antidepressants, can help weaken alcoholics' urge to drink (NIAAA-sponsored research has already shown that lithium, an antidepressant, does not affect alcoholism).

- better understand brain regions that control alcohol craving and drinking behavior.

About 20 percent of adults who go to doctors have had an

alcohol problem at one time. Yet doctors often do not recognize the alcoholism or recommend treatment. So researchers are developing tests for doctors to help them determine if their patients are abusing alcohol. Scientists also hope to develop laboratory tests to screen people for alcoholism.

Prevention

In the United States, prevention works to reduce the problems of occasional drinkers as well as those who drink a lot. No one prevention method reaches all people. Some have led to mixed results. For example, scare tactics, or trying to make someone be afraid of the negative consequences of drinking, seldom work. Also, Prohibition in the United States did not stop the making of alcohol or its consumption.

Today, law enforcement officers, the federal government, health professionals, teachers, businesspeople, and parents are all involved in various prevention methods. Some of their efforts include informing and educating people about alcohol and its effects, changing how and when people drink, and limiting the availability of alcoholic beverages.

Parents Parents are often the best source of alcohol information for children and teens. Children who become responsible drinkers generally come from families where alcohol is not the focus of events or activities. The best education parents can give is to set good examples and to not use alcohol to cope with problems. "If parents don't drink, the children probably won't," said Dr. Derek Miller, a professor of adolescent psychiatry at Northwestern University.

He continued, "Parents are far too casual about kids' use of alcohol. Parties are still going on with kegs of beer that parents have colluded in—if they haven't provided them outright. Even if parents stay home when children are having parties, they hide out in the basement and don't supervise."[3]

"Some parents would hide in their house when we'd have our drinking parties," remembers Keith Schooler, age twenty-seven, of his teen years in Indianapolis, Indiana. "Sometimes they'd say to us, 'I'd rather see you guys here getting drunk than getting drunk and driving around.' When we were too drunk to drive, we'd crash at a friend's house. But some of us still drove after we had too much to drink."[4]

Parents need to set firm guidelines about their expectations. For example, underage (under twenty-one) drinking is illegal in all states. Parents can inform their teens of this law, then state their own guidelines and rules about alcohol. According to a study of about 11,000 students, teens were less likely to use alcohol if their parents disapproved.

Parents can also sponsor or chaperon alcohol-free and drug-free activities. This includes parties, team banquets, dances, tournaments, and other group events. They could take groups of teens ice skating, roller skating, and bowling.

Schools and Communities Most schools offer drug education programs for elementary, junior, and senior high school students. Some schools target younger children, including first- and second-grade students. One grandmother was surprised when her grandson talked about his kindergarten alcohol and drug program. "Brian said he'd write us up and report us to his teacher if he caught us drinking or smoking," she said.[5]

These programs are often for students who do not yet have an alcohol or drug problem. They inform students about alcohol

91

and alcoholism, help develop good problem-solving skills, and build self-esteem.

One highly praised school program is called Discovery: Positive Connections for Kids. Teachers lead fifth- through eighth-grade students through discussions, role-playing, and activity worksheets. Posters and audio and videotapes are also used. The program helps students increase self-esteem, learn ways to deal with peer pressure, and develop positive ways to cope with problems. Discovery also helps children of alcoholics (COAs) learn how to cope with an alcoholic parent.

Schools have developed their own no-alcohol programs. One high school student in Utah described a novel no-alcohol and no-drug approach at her school. "We have trading cards for the school's sports teams to promote being drug free. The players on the card must be drug free. Kids at all schools really look up to the sports players. They want to be like them. The players set a great example for the kids."[6]

Schools have also sponsored alcohol-free parties. One teen in Iowa said her high school has "had many successful nonalcohol and drug-free parties. One consisted of a hay ride, barn dance, and bonfire. Another party had many different activities, such as a volleyball tournament, movies, board games, and pizza and pop."[7] Another teen said that on graduation night, her "high school, along with numerous others throughout the community, sponsors a drug-free, nonalcohol party called Project Graduation.[8]

Nike, Inc., the manufacturer of sports tennis shoes, offers support for drug- and alcohol-free graduation parties. The company donates a product to be used as a raffle item or door prize at graduation events.

One of the toughest gangs in America.

 **Clubs**

Just Say No clubs help teens develop skills to resist using alcohol and other drugs. Thousands of clubs are thriving across the United States.

Alcohol

In 1976, people in Boston started an alcohol-free New Year's celebration called First Night. Community people sing, dance, carve ice sculptures, tell stories, and play music. Fireworks often end the evening. Many events are geared toward families. Today, ninety-one cities, from Toronto to Honolulu, hold First Night festivals.

Youth Groups Attending self-help groups, such as Alateen, can help teens make choices about alcohol use. Alateen also provides peer support for COA teens.

Young people can also join various prevention groups. In Minneapolis and St. Paul, Minnesota, Native American young people can attend Soaring Eagles, a drug abuse prevention program. Jackie Dionne, the youth coordinator, said that Soaring Eagles "develops leadership skills through activities and learning opportunities."[9] Anyone from age three to twenty can attend. Soaring Eagles offers discussion groups on drugs and alcohol, family retreats, and field trips.

Those seven to fourteen years old can join Just Say No clubs. There are now more than 13,000 clubs across the United States. The goal of Just Say No is to "help young people help themselves."[10] Members promise not to drink or use other drugs.

Questions For Discussion

1. Everyone faces some problems in life. What are some things that help people overcome their problems?

2. What are some nonalcohol and drug-free ways that you feel good?

3. Physical activity, such as walking, jogging, or dancing, can produce a natural "high." Why?

7

Drunk Driving, Pregnancy, and Alcohol

Two serious teen alcohol problems that stand out today are drunk driving, and drinking during pregnancy, which can result in a baby born with fetal alcohol syndrome (FAS). Both issues have received much attention on television and radio and in newspapers and school programs.

Teenagers and Drunk Driving

Alarming Drinking and Driving Statistics In a recent Gallup Organization survey, Americans said drunk driving was the number-one problem on highways. Drinking and driving statistics in the United States show why. Traffic crashes involving drunk drivers are the number-one killer of people aged five to twenty-two. Someone is killed by a drunk driver every twenty-four minutes.

In 1992, 20,000 people were killed and 197,000 were injured in alcohol-related traffic crashes. This cost Americans more than $57 billion in property damage, medical emergency services, lost wages, travel delay, and legal costs. About 60 percent of young people involved had alcohol in their blood, and over 40 percent were legally drunk at the time of the car accident.

Two in every five Americans will be involved in an alcohol-related car crash sometime in their lives. So, in a room of twenty-five people, ten will eventually suffer an alcohol-related crash. Over one third of young people killed in such crashes were not drinking. Instead, they were being driven by someone who had been drinking.

Measuring Intoxication In the United States, the legal method for measuring intoxication is called blood alcohol content or BAC. It is a measure of how much alcohol, by percent, is in someone's blood. A BAC of 0.10 percent means that for every 1,000 drops of blood, there is 1 drop of alcohol.

Although a BAC of 0.10 seems low, it is the legal definition of intoxication in forty-five states. Because people drive poorly with even lower BACs, as of 1993, five states—California, Maine, Oregon, Utah, and Vermont—have lowered their BAC standard to 0.08.

This table shows how different BAC levels affect drinkers' behaviors or feelings.

BAC	Behavior or Feelings
0.01 – 0.04	Relaxed, some loss of inhibition, talks more, judgment and reaction time somewhat impaired.
0.05 – 0.07	Coordination decreases, may stumble or slip, may slur words, reaction time slower.
0.08 – 0.11	Impaired or poor sense of judgment, loss of inhibition, poor decision-making, slurred words, blurry vision, clumsy. At a *BAC of 0.10* a drinker is six times more likely to have a driving accident, than a non-drinker.
0.12 – 0.15	Staggers, very sleepy, little control over emotions. At *0.15 BAC*, a drinker is twenty-five times more likely to have a driving accident than a non-drinker.
0.16 – 0.20	Cannot coordinate movements, may cry without restraint, laugh hysterically or become enraged.
0.30	Confused, cannot understand people or events; may pass out.
0.40	Often goes into a coma and requires the use of oxygen.
0.50	Breathing or heart stops. Death often results. About 1,000 people die this way every year.

Teen Drinking and Driving

It is illegal for people under twenty-one years of age to drink. The U.S. National Highway Transportation and Safety Administration estimates that this law has saved over 12,000 lives since it began in 1975 and has reduced teen traffic deaths by 13 percent.

To further reduce teen traffic crashes, the National Transportation Safety Board recommends that all states take away the licenses of teens testing BAC positive (anything at or over 0.10 BAC) and not allow 16- and 17-year-olds to drive between midnight and 5:00 A.M. This is when most drunken driving deaths occur. Those who work at night or need to travel could, however, still drive with special permission. So far, eight states have enforced these laws for 15- to 17-year-olds.

Teens often view drinking and driving as important because they believe it shows that they are mature. Driving gives teens a sense of power and freedom. However, because teens do not have the adult experience of driving, they may not handle a car well. This is especially true in an impending accident.[1]

Teens drink and drive for many reasons. They may not realize how alcohol has affected their behavior and feelings. They may be influenced by peers. Or they may believe that they are invincible, that nothing bad will happen to them.[2] The results of alcohol-related crashes are often worse if seat belts are not worn, and many teens do not wear their seat belts.

"Some kids don't think ahead when they drink, then drive," said Jake Trippel, a senior at White Bear Lake, Minnesota, High School. "For example, they'll go to a party, hoping that someone there isn't drinking, so they can get a ride home later."

He continued, "Some kids, a small percentage, think they drive better if they've had some drinks. They believe they drive slower and are more aware. Of course that's not true."[3]

If teens are caught driving while intoxicated (DWI) or driving under the influence (DUI), here is what happens: Police or highway patrol officers can stop a teen driver suspected of being drunk. They can ask the teen to take field sobriety tests, such as walking in a straight line, touching the nose with a finger, or counting. Officers will also use a breath test to quickly and accurately measure BAC.

If the BAC is at or above the legal limit, officers will arrest the teen for DWI or DUI. If the teen refuses to test for BAC, his or her license will be lost, even if he or she is not guilty of DWI. If officers feel that a teen's driving is dangerous due to alcohol, they will charge a DWI, even if the BAC is as low as 0.06.[4]

Once a teen is arrested, his or her car is towed and stored, and the teen must pay a fee to get it back. After the teen is fingerprinted, the parents are called to take their son or daughter home. Sometimes parents have to pay bail bond fees for release of their teen.

Teens found guilty of DWI can lose their licenses for anywhere from ninety days to a year. They also pay a fee to get their licenses back. A DWI on their record may also cause their auto insurance costs to increase. Some companies will cancel the insurance policy. The family must then buy high-risk auto insurance, which usually costs more. Teens may also have to pay fines, or be sent to alcohol education classes, which they must pay for. Driving while intoxicated is a crime and will stay on a teen's record.

Protection for Teens from Drunk Drivers

To protect themselves from drunk drivers, teens can:

- Decide before going to a party or an event who will drive home. The driver then does not drink at all or drinks only very little. Some businesses offer free soft drinks to these designated drivers.

- Report drunk-driving suspects. Many communities have special telephone numbers to report possible drunken drivers.

- Not allow someone who is drunk to drive home. Drinkers may not realize how drunk they are. Alcohol interferes with their judgment. Taking a drunk driver's car keys away may save lives.

- Keep away from possible drunk drivers on the road. If teens suspect a driver is drunk, they can pull over. Signs of a drunk driver include a car speeding, wandering from lane to lane, making abrupt stops or starts, and using wrong or no signals.

- Never ride with a drunk driver. Nearly one-third of teens say they have. Be sure friends have a sober ride home. Call a taxi if necessary.

Prevention and Education

Students Against Drunk Driving (SADD) membership is open to all teens. It was founded in 1981 by a Wayland, Massachusetts, high school coach and administrator, Robert Anastas, and his students, and now has 7 million members in 25,000 chapters worldwide. There are SADD chapters for middle school, high school, and college students. The organization estimates saving an average of ten lives a day for the last ten years.

Students Against Drunk Driving encourages young people not to drink or use drugs. Teens who join SADD sign a contract with their parents. Under the contract, teens promise to call their parents for a ride home if the driver has been drinking or using drugs. Parents agree to pay for a taxi or drive their teens home, at any time, any place, without questions or punishment.

Educating students about making alcohol and drug decisions is also an objective of SADD. One teen in Solon, Ohio, is involved with her high school SADD chapter. She attends monthly SADD meetings, where a speaker talks about personal experiences with alcohol or drug abuse or about effective programs. Students ask questions at the end of each meeting. This student finds that SADD "reinforces the importance of a drug and alcohol free life."[5]

Mothers Against Drunk Driving (MADD) was founded in California in 1980 by a woman named Candy Lightner after her thirteen-year-old daughter was killed by a drunk hit-and-run driver. Today, MADD consists of nearly 3 million members in 400 chapters worldwide. Membership is open to anyone. MADD focuses on finding solutions to drunk driving and underage drinking problems. MADD also offers support to those who have suffered because of drunk drivers.

In the United States, MADD has helped enact more than 1,250 drunk driving laws. It is responsible for the underage drinking law in all states and for the law in most states that people who fail or refuse to take a BAC test lose their licenses.

Anheuser-Busch in St. Louis, Missouri, offers programs in

Ever Get Somebody Totally Wasted?

TAKE THE KEYS.
CALL A CAB.
TAKE A STAND.

FRIENDS DON'T LET FRIENDS DRIVE DRUNK

Posters like this help spread the message: do not ride with a drunken driver.

communities across the United States. One high-school program, "Make the Right Call," features Barbara Baab. As a registered nurse who cared for trauma victims, Baab tells vivid stories of her experiences. She focuses on underage drinking and drunk driving.

Baab "tells teens that they have the power, as well as the responsibility, to make choices. She aims to dispel the invincible, 'it can't happen to me' attitude that many teens have and drives home the fact that underage drinking and drunk driving are serious issues with serious consequences."[6]

Other programs focus on teens talking with other teens about the consequences of drinking and driving. One successful program in Malvern, Pennsylvania, is run by the Bryn Mawr Rehabilitation Hospital. The program called Cruisin' not Boozin' brings teens who have suffered brain injuries in alcohol-related crashes together with other high school students.

One Cruisin' not Boozin' volunteer is Steve Zandy, now twenty-two years old. His story started at age eleven, when he took his first drink. He tells his listeners, "When I got drunk, I thought I could do anything." At age fifteen, while drunk one night, he smashed his sister's car into a tree. He was in a coma for two months after the accident. His brain was permanently damaged. Only through intensive therapy has he relearned to swallow, walk, and talk. His story always shakes his teen listeners.[7]

Teen Drinking and Pregnancy

In the United States, teen pregnancies are increasing. Today, teen mothers have more than 25 percent of all babies born each year. About 1.1 million teens get pregnant each year. That is about five teen girls out of every fifty. The number of teens under fifteen years of age who get pregnant is rising. Eight out of ten of these teens say their pregnancies were not planned.

About half of pregnant teens give birth. The others lose their babies by miscarriages or choose to have abortions. About 400,000 choose abortion during the first few months. Babies born to teen mothers in any given year will cost Americans more than $7 billion over the next twenty years.[8]

Drinking while pregnant When a pregnant teen drinks, the alcohol crosses the placenta. The placenta develops during pregnancy and connects the baby's umbilical cord to the mother for food and oxygen. Soon after the baby's birth, the mother's body eliminates the placenta.

The alcohol that moves across the placenta is the same strength or concentration as it is in the mother's bloodstream. However, the effect on the unborn baby is greater than on the mother because the baby is so much smaller. So when a mother drinks, the unborn baby drinks as well.

Research shows that alcohol harms the baby the most during the first three months of pregnancy. An unborn baby can be affected by alcohol even before a teen tests positive for pregnancy. Since most teen pregnancies are unplanned, teen mothers who drink may not know they are pregnant.

Binge drinking—drinking five or more drinks in less than an hour—can greatly harm the fetus or unborn baby. The more drinks consumed in a short time, the longer it takes the mother's body to process and eliminate the alcohol. However, teens or adults can eliminate alcohol much faster than a small fetus or unborn baby. The fetus' organs are immature and smaller. So the alcohol stays in the baby's body much longer than in the mother's.

Milk is one of the best drinks for both mother and baby. However, some alcoholic teen mothers prefer to drink alcohol. Whatever the mother drinks, the baby also drinks.

What can happen to a baby if the mother drinks
Alcohol is a toxin, or a poison, to a developing baby. It is a substance that can cause birth defects. No one knows how many babies born to teens are harmed because the mother drank alcohol while pregnant.

We do know that drinking during pregnancy increases the risk of miscarriage, stillbirth, and early infant death. Drinking mothers may deliver small or premature babies. Low birth weight is the main cause of death, disability, and illness among newborns. Teen mothers are more likely to have small babies. Also, many pregnant teens do not eat healthy diets or get good health care. This will have a direct effect on a developing fetus.

Fetal Alcohol Syndrome and Fetal Alcohol Effects Not all women who drink alcohol during pregnancy deliver babies with serious birth defects. However, pregnant women who drink are more likely to harm their unborn babies. Their babies can have Fetal Alcohol Syndrome (FAS) or Fetal Alcohol Effects (FAE). FAS babies have more severe problems than FAE babies.

FAS babies may have any or all of the following symptoms:

- Small heads.

- Deformed faces, hands, or feet.

- Heart, liver, and kidney problems.

- Sight and hearing problems.

- Slow growth and poor coordination.

- Below-average intelligence (sometimes parts of their brains are poorly developed or missing).

107

Some FAS babies are so badly damaged they die after birth. FAS babies also are sometimes overactive. They may have behavior and learning problems and will suffer these problems all their lives. There is no known cure for the effects of fetal alcohol syndrome.

FAE babies may also have stunted growth and below-average intelligence. They may be small and restless. Their faces may look all right, but they may have crooked toes, or ears that stick out. Like FAS problems, FAE problems cannot be reversed.

Even with special care after birth, FAS and FAE babies will never catch up. As FAS and FAE children grow, they continue to show alcohol-related problems. These include short attention spans, poor judgment, inability to learn from experience, and poor memories. Sometimes frustrated FAE teens drop out of school or cannot hold a job.

"What's really sad is how many FAS and FAE kids go through life undetected," said Ann Streissguth of the University of Washington. She specializes in FAS behavior. "It takes a trained eye to spot FAS. And in FAE, mildly retarded kids are often misjudged because they tend to be talkative and outgoing. No one dreams their nervous systems are damaged."[9]

Fetal Alcohol Syndrome is the third-leading cause of mental retardation in newborns. Researchers do not know how many FAE children are mentally retarded. In the United States, 5,000 FAS babies and 50,000 FAE babies are born each year.[10]

FAS and FAE prevention Since the early 1700s, doctors and researchers in England and France have reported on alcohol's harmful effects on unborn babies. In 1973, a group of scientists first came up with the term "Fetal Alcohol Syndrome" to describe certain patterns of birth defects. Originally, scientists linked FAS with the poor diet of drinking mothers. Researchers now know that drinking alcohol itself during pregnancy causes FAS and FAE. Many doctors worldwide have since reported on FAS babies born to drinking mothers.

Since 1973, society's awareness of FAS and FAE has increased. Researchers estimate that FAS treatment costs in the United States are nearly a third of a billion dollars each year. One statistic continues to puzzle researchers: FAS in African-American babies is nearly seven times higher than that in white babies. Researchers think that genes, or heredity, may cause this higher rate but do not know for sure.[11]

To increase public awareness of FAS, the federal government in 1989 ruled that all alcoholic beverage containers must warn of the risks of drinking while pregnant. Despite all educational efforts, the National Institute on Drug Abuse recently found that "only 55 percent of women of childbearing age have heard of fetal alcohol syndrome."[12]

Actress Joanne Woodward used a television movie to reach millions of viewers about the hazards of drinking and taking drugs during pregnancy. The movie, *Blind Spot*, first aired in 1993. It featured a group home where substance-abusing mothers can have their babies and then stay there with them for nearly a year. During their stay, they learn about parenting and the effects of drugs and alcohol.

"Previously," said Woodward, "if a baby tested positive for drugs or alcohol, it was taken away and put in foster care. The mother lost any hope of bonding—and the motivation it gives her to keep off drugs."[13] The movie was modeled after a home in Middletown, Connecticut. However, few of these homes exist in the United States today.

Questions For Discussion

1. Do you think night driving curfews violate teens' rights?

2. Some say that people who drink and drive have chosen to drive irresponsibly. What do you think?

3. Do you think a bartender or waiter should not serve alcohol to a pregnant woman? Why or why not?

4. Do you think jailing a mother whose baby was born drunk will help people understand the dangers of drinking while pregnant? Why or why not?

P.O. Box 800
Marlboro, MA 01752
Tel: 508-481-3568

Dear Parents,

Our children are faced with enormous decisions regarding the use or avoidance of alcohol and other drugs. I am an educator and parent of three young men, who understands your concerns about these issues. Despite our determination to provide a drug free environment, statistics and past experiences have proven that this is difficult to attain.

We should never give up. We must begin to deal with these problems with an improved perspective on relevant solutions. Our children often push us away in their desire to acquire independence as they mature. We are less a part of their intimate world. We hear these comments, "My world is different than yours" or "I can handle it" or "It's my business". It's no wonder that many of us are shocked when we discover that our children are using illegal substances. We learn sadly that yes, it can be our children. I am convinced that if you and your child work together to recognize how death has been camouflaged through poor parent-child communication and peer pressure, then you can strive towards eliminating death and injury caused by the use of illegal substances. Thus our new Contract for Life reflects the S.A.D.D. commitment to that challenge.

The Contract for Life acts as a safeguard against death. It helps to improve family communication and acts as a support for children as they cope with peer pressure when they are faced with the decision not to use illegal drugs or engage in underage drinking. When you use the Contract for Life you demonstrate that your love for your children and theirs for you is strong enough to overcome any obstacle that may force them to challenge death.

I urge all parents to team up with your local S.A.D.D. chapter. Your children need your help. The thousands of parents who have responded positively have proven that they can make a difference. Our children are most precious. Believe in them as they believe in you.

Let the dream continue.

Robert Anastas
Founder

FRIENDS DON'T LET FRIENDS DRIVE DRUNK

SADD and the SADD logo are registered with the United States Patent and Trademark Office. All rights reserved by S.A.D.D. — Students Against Driving Drunk, Inc. a Massachusetts non-profit corporation. Trademark registration is pending in other jurisdictions.

CONTRACT
FOR
LIFE

A Contract for Life
Between Parent and Teenager

Under this contract we understand S.A.D.D. encourages all youth to adopt a no use policy and obey the laws of their state with regards to alcohol and illicit drugs.

Teenager

I agree to call you for advice and/or transportation at any hour from any place if I am ever faced with a situation where a driver has been drinking or using illicit drugs. I have discussed with you and fully understand your attitude toward any involvement with underage drinking or the use of illegal drugs.

Signature _____

Parent

I agree to come and get you at any hour, any place, no questions asked and no argument at that time; or I will pay for a taxi to bring you home safely. I expect we would discuss this at a later time.
I agree to seek safe, sober transportation home if I am ever in a situation where I have had too much to drink or a friend who is driving me has had too much to drink.

Signature _____

Date _____

Distributed by S.A.D.D. "Students Against Driving Drunk"

Here is the SADD "Contract for Life" that teens and their parents sign. The letter above it explains to parents the importance of the contract.

Alateen: Is It for You?

Alateen is a support group for young people whose lives have been affected by someone else's drinking. The following twenty questions are meant to help you decide whether or not Alateen is for you.

1. Do you have a parent, close friend, or relative whose drinking upsets you?
2. Do you cover up your real feelings by pretending you don't care?
3. Does it seem as though every holiday is spoiled because of drinking?
4. Do you tell lies to cover up for someone else's drinking or what's happening in your home?
5. Do you stay out of the house as much as possible because you hate it there?
6. Are you afraid to upset someone for fear it will set off a drinking bout?
7. Do you feel nobody really loves you or cares what happens to you?
8. Are you afraid or embarrassed to bring your friends home?
9. Do you think the drinker's behavior is caused by you, other members of your family, friends, or rotten breaks in life?
10. Do you make threats such as "If you don't stop drinking, fighting, etc., I'll run away"?

11. Do you make promises about behavior such as "I'll get better school marks, go to church or keep my room clean" in exchange for a promise that the drinking and fighting stop?
12. Do you feel that if your mom or dad loved you, she or he would stop drinking?
13. Do you threaten or actually hurt yourself to scare your parents into saying, "I'm sorry," or "I love you"?
14. Do you believe no one could possibly understand how you feel?
15. Do you have money problems because of someone else's drinking?
16. Are mealtimes frequently delayed because of the drinker?
17. Have you considered calling the police because of drinking behavior?
18. Have you refused dates out of fear or anxiety?
19. Do you think that if the drinker stopped drinking, your other problems would be solved?
20. Do you ever treat people (teachers, schoolmates, teammates, etc.) unjustly because you are angry at someone else for drinking too much?

If you have answered yes to even some of these questions, Alateen may help you. You can contact Al-Anon or Alateen by looking in your local telephone directory or by writing to:

Al-Anon Family Group Headquarters, Inc.
P.O. Box 862
Midtown Station
New York, NY 10018
(800) 356-9996

Reprinted with permission of Al-Anon Family Group Headquarters, Inc.

Glossary

Acquired Immunodeficiency Syndrome (AIDS)—A deadly viral disease that destroys the ability of the body's immune system to protect itself.

addict—Someone who is dependent on or controlled by a drug.

alcohol—A liquid with no color or smell. One kind, ethyl alcohol (ethanol), is used to make alcoholic beverages.

alcoholic—Someone who needs, or is addicted to, alcohol.

alcoholic hepatitis—A painful liver inflammation, caused by prolonged, excessive drinking.

alcoholism—A disease in which a person's need to drink alcohol is strong and cannot be controlled.

Antabuse—A drug given by a doctor to stop an alcoholic from drinking. Antabuse and alcohol together produce serious reactions such as nausea, headaches, and vomiting.

binge drinking—Drinking five or more drinks in less than one hour.

blackout—A period of time when someone cannot remember a drinking episode. A person need not necessarily lose consciousness to black out. He or she just cannot remember things.

Blood Alcohol Content (BAC)—The measure of how much alcohol, by percent, is in someone's blood.

Children of Alcoholics (COAs)—Children of alcoholic parent(s).

cirrhosis—A permanent, dangerous disease that kills liver cells.

dealcoholized drinks—Drinks that have their alcohol removed after fermentation or brewing.

detox—Managing alcohol withdrawal (detoxification).

distillation—The process of producing strong alcoholic liquids from wine or beer.

Driving While Intoxicated (DWI) or Driving Under the Influence (DUI)—Point at which the law prohibits people from driving, if their blood alcohol content is above a predetermined limit.

ethanol—Also called ethyl alcohol; is a thin, colorless liquid with little or no odor. Used for alcoholic beverages and in many household products such as varnishes, paints, and cosmetics.

excretion—Elimination of alcohol through urine, breath, sweat, or saliva.

fatty liver—Extra fat in the liver. A fatty liver cannot process alcohol or other foods as fast as a healthy liver.

fermentation—The process of yeast breaking sugars into carbon dioxide and water.

Fetal Alcohol Effects (FAE)—Similar to Fetal Alcohol Syndrome, except that defects are not as severe.

Fetal Alcohol Syndrome (FAS)—A pattern of mental and physical defects in babies born to women who drank significant amounts of alcohol while pregnant.

fetus—An unborn, developing baby.

genetics—A branch of biology dealing with heredity.

hallucination—Imaginary sights, sounds, and smells, believed to be real.

hangover—A mild withdrawal from alcohol.

hieroglyphics—Writing in the form of pictures.

Human Immunodeficiency Virus (HIV)—The virus that causes AIDS.

intoxication—Drunkenness.

metabolism—The breakdown of food by the body.

miscarriage—The death of the fetus and its expulsion from the mother's uterus.

moderation—Drinking no more than two average drinks per day for men and one average drink per day for women.

moonshine—Homemade whiskey.

nutriholic drinks—Drinks made from fresh fruits, fruit juices, and very small amounts of alcohol.

osteoporosis—Weakened or brittle bones caused by a lack of calcium in the diet, or the inability of the body to absorb calcium.

pancreatitis—Inflammation of the pancreas, a serious and painful disease.

patent medicines—Fake drugs or remedies.

prescription—A doctor's orders or instructions for a drug.

prohibition—Provided for by the Eighteenth Amendment to the United States Constitution, which was in effect from 1919 to 1933. It prohibited sales, manufacture, import, export, and transport of alcoholic beverages in the United States.

recovering alcoholic—A nondrinking alcoholic. Because alcoholism cannot be cured, sober alcoholics say they are recovering.

relapse—Drinking again by a recovering alcoholic after a period of being sober.

stillbirth—A miscarriage after at least twenty weeks of pregnancy.

temperance—Moderation in drinking.

tippling houses—Public drinking places in colonial America.

tolerance—The process by which a body becomes used to a drug so that the drug no longer has an effect. An increased drug dose is then needed to get the same effect as the lower dose once provided.

tranquilizer—A drug that calms and relaxes.

umbilical cord—A flexible tube connecting the fetus from its navel to the mother's placenta. It has two arteries and a vein that feed the fetus and take away its wastes.

wine coolers—Sweet, syrupy alcoholic beverages made from fruit juice, sugar, and wine.

withdrawal—The process of ridding the body of alcohol.

Chapter Notes

Chapter 1

1. Boyd Gibbons, "Alcohol: The Legal Drug," *National Geographic* (February 1992), p. 7.

2. "Alcohol and Drug Consumption: Alcohol," *The New Enclyclopaedia Britannica*, Vol. 13, Macropaedia (Chicago: Encyclopaedia Britannica, 1985), p. 220.

3. As reported by Anne Kaplan, Marjorie Hoover, and Willard Moore, *The Minnesota Ethnic Food Book* (St. Paul, MN: Minnesota Historical Society Press, 1986), p. 77.

4. Nancy Nielsen, *Teen Alcoholism* (New York: Lucent Books, 1990), p. 22.

5. Gibbons, p. 11.

6. Judy Monroe, *The Facts About Prescription Drugs* (Mankato, MN: Crestwood House, 1988), pp. 7–8.

7. James Young, *The Toadstool Millionaires* (Princeton, N.J.: Princeton University Press, 1961), pp. 129–130.

8. "Corruption in the Saloon and Local Options Law," *The Bottom Line* (Fall, 1992), p. 15.

9. Ibid.

10. Nielsen, p. 29.

11. "A Sobering Reality," *Scholastic Update* (November 16, 1990), p. 2.

Chapter 2

1. Julie Johnsson, *Wine Coolers: The Uncool Coolers*, pamphlet (reprinted by Narcotics Education, Inc., 1991, from *Listen Magazine*), p.1.

2. Boyd Gibbons, "Alcohol: The Legal Drug," *National Geographic* (February, 1992), p. 33.

3. Harold McGee, *On Food and Cooking: The Science and Lore of the Kitchen* (New York: Scribner, 1984), p. 497.

4. Secretary of Health and Human Services, *Alcohol and Health: Seventh Special Report to the U.S. Congress* (Rockville, MD.: National Institute on Alcohol Abuse and Alcoholism, 1990), p. 123.

5. American Liver Foundation, *Alcohol and the Liver: Myth vs. Facts*, pamphlet (Cedar Grove, N.J.: American Liver Foundation, 1993).

6. National Council on Alcoholism, Inc., *Facts on Alcoholism and Alcohol-Related Problems*, fact sheet (November 1987).

7. The American Council for Drug Education, "Alcohol Use and Alcoholism," news release (March 1992).

8. Office for Substance Abuse Prevention, *The Discovery Kit: Program Manual* (Rockville, MD: Alcohol, Drug Abuse, and Mental Health Administration, U.S. Department of Health and Human Services, 1992), p. 5.

9. Secretary of Health and Human Services, p. 7.

Chapter 3

1. Ross Fishman, *The Encyclopedia of Psychoactive Drugs: Alcohol and Alcoholism* (New York: Chelsea House, 1986), pp. 21–22.

2. Secretary of Health and Human Services, *Alcohol and Health: Seventh Special Report to the U.S. Congress* (Rockville, MD.: National Institute on Alcohol Abuse and Alcoholism, 1990), p. xvii.

3. Al-Anon Family Group Headquarters, Inc., *Lois Remembers: Memoirs of the Co-Founder of Al-Anon and Wife of the Co-Founder of Alcoholics Anonymous* (New York: 1979), p. 91.

4. Jean Kinney and Gwen Leaton, *Loosening the Grip: A Handbook of Alcohol Information* (St. Louis, MO: Mosby Year Book, 1991), p. 17.

5. "A Sobering Reality," *Scholastic Update* (November 16, 1990), p. 2.

6. Life Skills Education, *Drinking Myths: The Real Facts, Not the Folklore*, booklet (Northfield, MN: 1991), p. 11.

7. Boyd Gibbons, "Alcohol: The Legal Drug," *National Geographic* (February, 1992), p. 33.

8. Nancy Nielsen, *Teen Alcoholism* (New York: Lucent Books, 1990), p. 79.

9. Michael Massing, "Mixed Messages," *Modern Maturity* (February/March, 1992), p. 38.

10. Nielsen, pp. 86-87.

11. Patricia Taylor, "Youth and Alcohol: Changing Attitudes," *The Challenge* (November/December 1989), p. 9.

12. Julia Siler, "It Isn't Miller Time Yet, and This Bud's Not for You," *Business Week* (June 24, 1991), p. 52.

13. Michael Jacobson et al., *The Booze Merchants* (Washington, D.C.: Center for Science in the Public Interest, 1983), p. 69.

14. Nielsen, p. 88.

15. Author interview with Jake Trippel, White Bear Lake, MN, (April 22, 1993).

16. "Growing Concern Over Alcohol Advertising," *Bottom Line* (Winter 1992), p. 15.

17. L. F. Cavazos, "Children and Drugs: How Drug Use Develops," *What Works: Schools Without Drugs* (Washington, D.C.: U.S. Department of Education, 1989), p. 7.

18. "Growing Concern Over Alcohol Advertising," p. 15.

19. Alan Luks and Joseph Barbato, *You Are What You Drink* (New York: Villard Books, 1989), p. 21.

Chapter 4

1. Jean Kinney and Gwen Leaton, *Loosening the Grip: A Handbook of Alcohol Information* (St. Louis, MO: Mosby Year Book, 1991), p. 319.

2. "Teen Alcohol Use Remains High," *ON TARGET* (September 1992), p. 6.

3. Daniel Anderson, "Many Factors Contribute to Youth Substance Abuse," *Minneapolis Star Tribune* (March 16, 1993), p. 2E.

4. Author interview with Jake Trippel, high school senior, (April 22, 1993).

5. Author interview with Keith Schooler, St. Paul, MN (May 3, 1993).

6. Author interview with Jake Trippel (April 22, 1993).

7. *Teenage Drinking*, pamphlet (Baltimore, MD: American Council on Alcoholism, Inc. 1992), p. 5.

8. Office for Substance Abuse, *Positive Connections for Kids: Program Manual* (Rockville, MD: U.S. Department of Health and Human Services, 1992), p. 23.

9. Boyd Gibbons, "Alcohol: The Legal Drug," *National Geographic,* (February 1992) p. 27.

10. Ibid., p. 28.

11. Ibid., p. 15.

12. Phil Sudo, "The Soviet Hangover," *Scholastic Update* (November 16, 1990), p. 14.

13. "Can You Stop People From Drinking?" *Journal Graphics, NOVA* transcript (show # 1919, air date: December 22, 1992), p. 1.

Chapter 5

1. Office for Substance Abuse, "The Fact Is Alcoholism Tends to Run

in Families," fact sheet (Washington, D.C.: Alcohol, Drug Abuse, and Mental Health Administration, U.S. Department of Public Health, 1991).

2. Al-Anon Family Group Headquarters, Inc., *Lois Remembers: Memoirs of the Co-Founder of Al-Anon and Wife of the Co-Founder of Alcoholics Anonymous* (New York: 1979), p. 22.

3. Boyd Gibbons, "Alcohol: The Legal Drug," *National Geographic* (February 1992), p. 25.

4. Jacqui Banaszynski, "Ties that Bind: Facing Up to the Family Secret," *Modern Maturity* (February/March, 1992), p. 33.

5. *Alcoholism in the Family: Is Everyone Trapped by the Bottle?* (San Bruno, CA.: Krames Communications, 1990), pp. 8–9.

6. Herbert L. Gravitz, *Recovery: A Guide for Adult Children of Alcoholics* (New York: Simon & Schuster, 1985), p. 21.

7. Office of Substance Abuse, *Prevention Guide: Children of Alcoholics* (Washington, D.C.: Department of Health and Human Services, U.S. Government Printing Office, 1991), p. 3.

8. Andrea Kaminski, *Mind-Altering Drugs: A Guide to the History, Uses, and Effects of Psychoactive Drugs* (Madison, WI.: Wisconsin Clearinghouse, 1992), p. 9.

9. Sandra R. Arbetter, "Children of Alcoholics," *Current Health 2* (February 1990), p. 15.

10. Al-Anon Family Group Headquarters, Inc., meeting table card, undated.

11. "Alcoholism Tends to Run in Families," pamphlet (Rockville, MD.: The National Association for Children of Alcoholics, n.d.)

Chapter 6

1. Al-Anon Family Group Headquarters, Inc., *Lois Remembers: Memoirs of the Co-Founder of Al-Anon and Wife of the Co-Founder of Alcoholics Anonymous,* (New York,: 1979), p. 145.

2. Laura McCarthy, "Beyond AA," *Health* (August 1991), p. 40.

3. Claire Safran, "Its Christmas Eve. Do You Know Where Your Children Are?" *Ladies Home Journal* (December 1991), p. 55.

4. Author Interview with Keith Schooler, St. Paul, MN. (May 3, 1993).

5. Author Interview with Carol Murray, St. Paul, MN. (April 12, 1993.)

6. "Query on Drug-Free Activities Prompts Many Student Opinions," *On TARGET,* (May, 1992), pp. 4-5.

7. Ibid.

8. "Query on Drug-Free Promotion Prompts Many Student Opinions," *On TARGET* (December 1992), p.5.

9. Richard Broderick, "The Red Road to Recovery," Minneapolis-St. Paul, MN. (January 1991), p. 136.

10. *"Just Say No" International 1991 Annual Report,* Oakland, CA.: "Just Say No" International, 1992, p. 15.

Chapter 7

1. *The Young Drinking Driver,* booklet (Northfield, MN.: Life Skills Education, 1992), p. 5.

2. *Youth Driving Without Impairment* (Washington, D.C.: National Commission Against Drunk Driving, 1989), p. viii.

3. Author Interview with Jake Trippel (April 22, 1993.)

4. *The Young Drunk Driver,* p. 11.

5. "Query on Drug Free Activities Prompts Many Student Opinions," *On TARGET,* (May, 1992), p. 4.

6. *Make the Right Call: A Program on Underage Drinking and Drunk Driving,* (Anheuser-Busch Companies Inc., 1992).

7. A.T. McPhee, "Teen Drunken Drivers Crash, Live, Tell," *Current Science* (February 28, 1992), pp. 4-5.

8. The Center for Population Options, "Teenage Pregnancy and Too-Early Child-Bearing: Public Costs, Personal Consequences," summary report, 1992, p. 2.

9. George Steinmetz, "The Preventable Tragedy: Fetal Acohol Syndrome," *National Geographic* (February 1992), p. 39.

10. March of Dimes Birth Defects Foundation, "Drinking During Pregnancy: Fetal Alcohol Syndrome and Fetal Alcohol Effects," information sheet (1991).

11. National Institute on Alcohol Abuse and Alcoholism, "Fetal Alcohol Syndrome," *Alcohol Alert* (Washington, D.C.: U.S. Government Printing Office, 1991), p. 2.

12. *Pregnant/Postpartum Women and Their Infants* (Office of Substance Abuse Prevention, Alcohol, Drug Abuse, and Mental Health Administration, June, 1991, p. 1.

13. "Woodward's Warning to Pregnant Women," *Parade Magazine,* (May 2, 1993) p. 17.

14. March of Dimes Birth Defects Foundation.

Further Reading

ORGANIZATIONS

Alcoholics Anonymous (AA)
Box 459
Grand Central Station
New York, NY 10163
(212) 870-3400
Teen booklets and pamphlets

**Al-Anon Family Group
Headquarters, Inc.**
P.O. Box 862
Midtown Station
New York, NY 10018
(212) 302-7240
Includes materials for both Alateen
and Al-Anon

Hazelden Foundation
15251 Pleasant Valley Road
P.O. Box 176
Center City, MN 55012-0176
(800) 328-9000
Many pamphlets, booklets, books,
and other materials for teens and
adults

The Health Connection
55 West Oak Ridge Drive
Hagerstown, MD 21740
(800) 548-8700
Pamphlets, booklets, books, and
other materials for teens and adults

Life Skills Education
314 Washington St.
Northfield, MN 55057
(800) 783-6743
Booklets for teens and adults

Johnson Institute
7205 Ohms Lane
Minneapolis, MN 55439
(800) 231-5165
Many pamphlets, booklets, books,
and other materials for teens and
adults

**National Clearinghouse for
Alcohol and Drug Information**
P.O. Box 2345
Rockville, MD 20847
(800) 729-6686
Publishes pamphlets, booklets,
books, and posters for teens and
adults

Wisconsin Clearinghouse
P.O. Box 1468
Madison, WI 53701
(800) 322-1468
Pamphlets, booklets, books, and
other materials for teens and adults

Titles For Teens

Almost All You Ever Wanted to Know about Alcohol but Didn't Know Who to Ask. Lansing, MI.: The Bottom Line, Alcohol Research Information Service, 1991.

Claypool, Jane, *Alcohol and You*. New York: Franklin Watts, 1988.

Different Like Me: A Book for Teens Who Worry about Their Parents' Use of Alcohol/Drugs. Madison, WI.: Wisconsin Clearinghouse, 1988.

Fishman, Ross. *The Encyclopedia of Psychoactive Drugs: Alcohol*. New York: Chelsea House Publishers, 1986.

Graeber, Laurel. *Are You Dying for a Drink?* New York: Messner, 1985.

Hyde, Margaret. *Alcohol: Uses and Abuses*. Hillside, N.J.: Enslow Publishers, 1988.

Nielsen, Nancy. *Teen Alcoholism*. New York: Lucent Books, 1990.

Ryan, Elizabeth. *Straight Talk about Drugs and Alcohol*. New York: Facts on File, 1989.

Ryerson, Eric. *When Your Parents Drink Too Much*. New York: Facts on File, 1985.

Seixas, Judith. *Living with a Parent Who Takes Drugs*. New York: Greenwillow Books, 1989.

Shuker, Nancy. *Everything You Need to Know about an Alcoholic Parent*. New York: Rosen Publishing, 1990.

Silverstein, Herma. *Alcoholism*. New York: Franklin Watts, 1990.

Stepney, Rob. *Alcohol*. New York: Franklin Watts, 1987.

Teens Talk about Alcohol and Alcoholism. Garden City, N.Y.: Doubleday, 1987.

Vogler, Roger, and Wayne Bartz. *Teenagers and Alcohol: When Saying No Isn't Enough*. Philadelphia: The Charles Press, 1992.

Ward, Brian. *Alcohol Abuse*. New York: Franklin Watts, 1989.

Where to Go for Help

Many organizations offer information about alcohol, treatment, and support for alcoholics, their families, and friends.

INFORMATION

SADD
P.O. Box 800
Marlboro, MA 01752
(508) 481-3568

MADD
P.O. Box 541688
Dallas, TX 75354
(214) 744-6233

National Clearinghouse for Alcohol and Drug Information
P.O. Box 2345
Rockville, MD 20852
(800) 729-6686

TARGET
P.O. Box 20626
11724 NW Plaza Circle
Kansas City, MO 64195
(800) 366-6667

National Council on Alcoholism, Inc.
12 West 21st Street
New York, NY 10010
(212) 206-6770

TREATMENT

Treatment Referral Hotline
(800) 662-4357
Refers anyone with an alcohol or drug problem to local counseling

Alcoholics Anonymous (AA)
P.O. Box 459
Grand Central Station
New York, NY 10163
(212) 870-3400

Rational Recovery
P.O. Box 800
Lotus, CA 95651
(916) 621-2667

Secular Organization for Sobriety (SOS)
Box 5
Buffalo, NY 14215
(716) 834-2922

Families Anonymous, Inc.
P.O. Box 528
Van Nuys, CA 91408
(310) 313-5800

Women for Sobriety
P.O. Box 618
Quakertown, PA 18951
(800) 333-1606

Look also in the yellow pages of your telephone book under "Alcoholism" or under "Drug Treatments." Or call your local public health department.

Support
Al-Anon Family Groups
Alateen
P.O. Box 862
Midtown Station
New York, NY 10018
(800) 344-2666

Children of Alcoholics Foundation
P.O. Box 4185
Grand Central Station
New York, NY 10163
(212) 754-0656

National Association for Children of Alcoholics
11426 Rockville Pike, Suite 100
Rockville, MD 20853
(301) 468-0985

Just Say No International
2101 Webster Street, Suite 1300
Oakland, CA 94612
(800) 258-2766

Index

A

AIDS, 31, 60
Al-Anon, 75, 77, 86, 87
Alateen, 75, 86, 87, 112
alcoholic hepatitis, 30
Alcoholics Anonymous (AA), 37,
    67, 80, 87
allergies, 26
American Council on Alcoholism,
    40, 60
American Medical Association, 37
American Temperance Union, 11
Anastas, Robert, 101
Antabuse, 84
Anti-Saloon League, 13
aqua vitae, 8
arthritis, 62

B

Beecher, Lyman, 11
binge drinking, 28, 58, 105
birth defects, 107, 108
blackout, 29, 71
blood alcohol content (BAC), 97,
    99, 100, 102
Bogart, Humphrey, 36
Booze Merchants, The, 44, 45
bourbon, 10
Brezhnev, Leonid, 64

C

cancer, 30
Capone, Al, 15
children of alcoholics (COAs),
    70-75, 77, 92, 94
cirrhosis, 30, 64
Clum, Dr. Franklin, 36, 37

cordials, 8

D

dealcoholized drinks, 49
detoxification (detox), 83, 86
diabetes, 62
Dionne, Jackie, 94
distillation, 7–8, 19
driving under the influence (DUI),
    100
driving while intoxicated (DWI),
    48, 100

E

Eighteenth Amendment, 13, 18
enzymes, 22
ethyl alcohol, 19, 20, 21
excretion, 22

F

Families Anonymous, 86
fatty liver, 30
Faulkner, William, 36
Federal Rehabilitation Act, 38
Federal Trade Commission, 46
fermentation, 5, 21
Fetal Alcohol Effects (FAE),
    107–109
Fetal Alcohol Syndrome (FAS),
    96, 107–109

G

Gorbachev, Mikhail, 64

H

hangover, 28–29
heart disease, 62

127

Hemingway, Ernest, 36
hieroglyphics, 6
Hostetter's Bitters, 11
hot toddy, 10
Huntington's disease, 68, 69

J
Jefferson, Thomas, 10
Just Say No, 94

K
Kilbourne, Dr. Jean, 44, 47, 88

L
Lewis, Sinclair, 36
Lightner, Candy, 102
lung disease, 62

M
metabolism, 21–22
miscarriage, 107
moonshining, 15
Mothers Against Drunk Driving
    (MADD), 102
Musto, Dr. David, 65
mutation, 64

N
Nation, Carrie A., 13
National Council on Alcoholism,
    33, 37
nonalcoholic drinks, 49
nutriholic drinks, 49

O
O'Neil, Eugene, 36
osteoporosis, 32

P
pancreatitis, 30
Passover, 9
patent medicines, 10, 11
placenta, 105

Prohibition, 13–14, 36, 90
"proof", 20
Puritans, 9

R
Rational Recovery, 88
Roosevelt, Franklin, 15

S
Secular Organization for Sobriety,
    88
Smith, Dr. Robert, 36
Soaring Eagles, 94
Steinbeck, John, 36
stillbirth, 107
Students Against Drunk Driving
    (SADD), 101, 102
sugar fungi, 5, 21

T
temperance, 11, 13
tippling houses, 10
tolerance, 24
toxin, 22, 107
tranquilizers, 27, 84
Twenty-first Amendment, 15

W
whiskey, 8, 10, 22
Willard, Frances, 13
Wilson, Bill, 37, 67
Wilson, Lois, 79
wine cooler, 20–22, 58
withdrawal, 84
Women for Sobriety, 88
Women's Christian Temperance
    Union, 13
Woodward, Joanne, 109

Y
yeast fungi, 21